Independent Schools
Examinations Board

HISTORY
ISEB Revision Guide

Medieval Realms: Britain 1066–1485
The Making of the United Kingdom: 1485–1750
Britain 1750–c.1900

Ed Adams

Independent Schools
Examinations Board

www.galorepark.co.uk

GALORE PARK

Published by ISEB Publications, an imprint of Galore Park Publishing Ltd
19/21 Sayers Lane, Tenterden, Kent TN30 6BW
www.galorepark.co.uk

Text copyright © Ed Adams 2009 and 2012

The right of Ed Adams to be identified as the author of this work has been
asserted by him in accordance with sections 77 and 78 of the Copyright,
Designs and Patents Act 1988.

Design and typesetting by Typetechnique

Illustrations by Gwyneth Williamson, Simon Tegg, Ian Moores and Ian Douglass

Printed by Lego S.p.A., Italy

ISBN: 978 1 907047 74 9

First edition published 2009, reprinted August 2009, 2010, 2011
Second edition published March 2012

Details of other ISEB Revision Guides for Common Entrance, examination
papers and Galore Park publications are available at www.galorepark.co.uk

Front cover illustration: Agriculture, 1934 (oil on canvas) by Dottori, Gerardo
(1884–1977) Galleria Nazionale d'Arte Moderna, Rome, Italy. Su concessione
del Ministero per i Beni e le Attività Culturali. Alinari/The Bridgeman
Art Library

About the author

Ed Adams was educated at Sutton Valence School and the University of Exeter, where he gained degrees in Law and Medieval Studies. He lives in Kent.

Acknowledgements

I would like to thank all the staff at Galore Park for helping to make this possible, and most especially Frances and Emily.

Contents

Introduction

This revision guide covers all three periods of the ISEB History syllabus for Common Entrance at 13+.

The material is arranged according to the structure set out in Galore Park's *So you really want to learn History* series, following a strictly chronological format. This, we believe, is the clearest, simplest and most useful way of learning the subject, and we hope it works for you.

This book will give you all the facts you need to know, and you should learn them thoroughly, but your success in the exam will depend on what you do with these facts. Do read the section below, which will give you advice on how to write strong answers in the exam and how to revise most effectively.

You will also find many opportunities throughout this book to test both your knowledge of the facts and your skill at writing answers.

History is a fascinating subject but has gained a reputation for being one of the harder ones to tackle. It can certainly be challenging, but need not be impossible. A good grasp of the skills that make a good historian will show your future teachers – and perhaps, future employers – that you have the necessary discipline to succeed in plenty of areas.

So make the most of this opportunity to show them. Good luck!

The syllabus and your exams

For Common Entrance History, you will sit an exam lasting an hour, for which you will need to answer one question from Part A and one question from Part B.

Part A: the evidence question

- The evidence question is worth 20 marks and it is recommended that you spend 20 minutes writing your answer to it.

- You will be presented with three sources. These may include an entry from a historical chronicle, an extract from a book written by a modern historian or a piece of correspondence from the time. At least one of the sources will be a picture, either produced at the time or a modern reconstruction.

- The first question will ask you to look at the first source and describe what the source is telling you.

- The second question will ask you to look at the second source and describe what the source is telling you in a little more detail.

- The third question will ask you to compare two of the sources and describe where the sources say different things.

- The fourth question will ask you to look at all the sources. It may ask you to give your opinion on which source is the most reliable. To answer this effectively you will need to understand the issues of **provenance**, **first-hand evidence** and **hindsight**.

- **Provenance** is the issue of where a source comes from. An account of the Battle of Hastings written by a Norman source would be very different from one written by an English source. A Norman author would write from a winner's perspective. He might exaggerate the bravery and skill of the Norman soldiers, or the cowardice and incompetence of the English. An English writer would write from a loser's perspective, and might argue that the Normans won purely by luck and that the battle was a great tragedy for England.

- **First-hand evidence** is that produced by an author who was actually present at the events described. An author who actually fought at the Battle of Hastings might write differently from an author who heard about the battle from another person. Sometimes authors write based on folk tales that have been passed through hundreds of people. Detail can be lost and exaggerations added. But a story that has been passed on before being written down may still have important things to say about another person's perception of events.

- **Hindsight** is the knowledge gained about an event after it has taken place. An author writing on the day after the Battle of Hastings might write differently from an author writing a hundred or even a thousand years later, who does so with the benefit of hindsight. Sometimes details may be forgotten or changed over time. But don't assume that a source will always be less reliable because a lot of time has passed. Modern historians – who generally write a long time after the event – can have a better overall view of the historical events.

- When you consider each source for the fourth question, you will need to look at these issues and see which ones are relevant. It is important to remember that there is often no 'right' or 'wrong' answer. You are being asked to argue your opinion, based on the evidence presented.

- You will not be asked for historical facts about the topic the sources refer to. But it may help you to give a strong, full answer if you know at least a little about the topic, for example, the background to it, the events of the time and any future consequences.

Part B: the essay question

- The essay question is worth 30 marks and it is recommended that you spend 35 minutes on it. There are two parts to the question: the **narrative essay** and the **analytical essay**.

- The **narrative essay** (worth 20 marks) will ask you to describe an event or events. You will need to be able to remember the historical facts and re-tell them in an understandable way.

- You should make sure that your answer has a sentence or two of introduction, a few paragraphs that describe the events and another sentence or two in conclusion.

- It will help to include the dates of the events you describe. This will prove to the examiner that you have learnt the material properly and will earn you more marks.

- You should write your answer in the past tense.

- You should not include any of your personal opinions: that comes in the next part.

- The **analytical essay** (worth 10 marks) will ask you to explain the reasons for something. You will need to consider why something happened and state your opinion, using sources to back up your claims.

- You should not waste time re-telling the events, as this will not earn you any marks. You need to look at the causes behind the event or the consequences of it.

- You will earn most marks for giving a balanced opinion. Try to argue two different opinions, then come to a conclusion where you reject one in favour of the other.

- There is never a 'right' or 'wrong' answer, only 'strong' and 'weak' ones. Another pupil could arrive at a completely different conclusion and receive the same number of marks. The examiner is looking for evidence that you understand the causes or consequences of an event, know how to analyse them properly and can back up your analysis by reference to the sources.

- When using historical sources to back up your claims, make sure you consider how reliable they are by considering provenance, first-hand evidence and hindsight. This could affect your conclusion.

Tips on revising

Get the best out of your brain

- Give your brain plenty of oxygen by exercising. You can revise effectively if you feel fit and well.

- Eat healthy food while you are revising. Your brain works better when you give it good fuel.

- Think positively. Give your brain positive messages so that it will want to study.

- Keep calm. If your brain is stressed it will not operate effectively.

- Take regular breaks during your study time.

- Get enough sleep. Your brain will carry on sorting out what you have revised while you sleep.

Get the most from your revision

- Don't work for hours without a break. Revise for 20–30 minutes then take a five-minute break.

- Do good things in your breaks: listen to your favourite music, eat healthy food, drink some water, do some exercise and juggle. Don't read a book, watch TV or play on the computer; it will conflict with what your brain is trying to learn.

- When you go back to your revision review what you have just learnt.

- Regularly review the facts you have learnt.

Get motivated

- Set yourself some goals and promise yourself a treat when the exams are over.

- Make the most of all the expertise and talent available to you at school and at home. If you don't understand something ask your teacher to explain.

- Get organised. Find a quiet place to revise and make sure you have all the equipment you need.

- Use year and weekly planners to help you organise your time so that you revise all subjects equally. (Available for download from www.galorepark.co.uk)

- Use topic and subject checklists to help you keep on top of what you are revising. (Available for download from www.galorepark.co.uk)

Know what to expect in the exam

- Use past papers to familiarise yourself with the format of the exam.

- Make sure you understand the language examiners use.

Before the exam

- Have all your equipment and pens ready the night before.

- Make sure you are at your best by getting a good night's sleep before the exam.

- Have a good breakfast in the morning.

- Take some water into the exam if you are allowed.

- Think positively and keep calm.

During the exam

- Have a watch on your desk. Work out how much time you need to allocate to each question and try to stick to it.

- Make sure you read and understand the instructions and rules on the front of the exam paper.

- Allow some time at the start to read and consider the questions carefully before writing anything.

- Read all the questions at least twice. Don't rush into answering before you have a chance to think about it.

- If a question is particularly hard move on to the next one. Go back to it if you have time at the end.

- Check your answers make sense if you have time at the end.

How to use this book

- Throughout this book you will see grey boxes marked with a ✓. These will give you suggestions about different tools you can use to help you remember the key facts/events/dates, etc. Everybody learns differently and these boxes will give you some ideas on different approaches you can use. However, they are only suggestions, but hopefully they will help you think of different ways that work for you. All these tips are taken from *Study Skills* by Elizabeth Holtom, published by Galore Park, and you can get details of all the different suggestions, as well as finding out what sort of learner you are, from this book.

- Read a page of this book, then cover it up and write down as many of the ideas as you can remember. Then look at the page again.

- Once you have finished reading a chapter, try the 'Test yourself' questions. This will show whether you have remembered the historical facts. Check your answers against those at the back of the book. Keep doing this over time to check that you have retained the information.

- Try the sample essay questions. These are written in exactly the same way as the questions in the exam. Suggested answers are given at the back of the book.

- Use the family trees (see pages 196–202) to see how the important historical figures are related to each other. This will help you to understand the tricky issues surrounding royal succession.

- Practice makes perfect, so get a copy of *History Practice Exercises 13+*, published by Galore Park. It contains over a hundred evidence and essay questions, giving you plenty of opportunity to develop your answer-writing skills.

For more tips on how to get the best from your revision and your exams, see *Study Skills* by Elizabeth Holtom, published by Galore Park.

Useful resources

Study Skills by Elizabeth Holtom
ISBN: 9781902984599

So you really want to learn History Book 1 by Bob Pace
ISBN: 9781905735013

So you really want to learn History Book 1 Answer Book by Bob Pace
ISBN 9781905735068

So you really want to learn History Book 2 by Nicholas Oulton
ISBN: 9781905735020

So you really want to learn History Book 2 Answer Book by David Sharp
ISBN: 9781905735075

So you really want to learn History Book 3 by Bob Pace
ISBN: 9781905735365

So you really want to learn History Book 3 Answer Book by Bob Pace
ISBN: 9781905735570

History Practice Exercises 13+ by Gavin Hannah and Paul Spencer
ISBN: 9780903627771

History Practice Exercises 13+ Answer Book by Gavin Hannah
ISBN: 9781907047008

All available from Galore Park: www.galorepark.co.uk

Part A: Medieval Realms: Britain 1066–1485

Chapter 1: The Norman Conquest

1.1 Background to the Conquest

On the death of Edward the Confessor on 5th January 1066, three men claimed the crown of England:

- Harold Godwinson

- William, Duke of Normandy

- Harald Hardrada, King of Norway

Harold Godwinson

- The largest landholder in England and Edward's most powerful noble.

- Harold claimed that Edward had named him as his successor on his deathbed.

- The *Anglo-Saxon Chronicle* supports Harold's claim: '*The prudent King [Edward] had settled the kingdom on high-born men, on Harold himself, the noble Earl.*'

William, Duke of Normandy

- The illegitimate son of Robert, Duke of Normandy, and distant cousin of Edward.

- William claimed that Edward had promised him the throne on a visit to England in 1052.

- William also claimed that Harold had sworn an oath over holy relics that he would support William's right to the English throne.

Harald Hardrada, King of Norway

- Harald was the King of Norway. He was supported by Harold's brother Tostig.

- Tostig argued that the English throne should have passed to King Magnus of Norway and then Hardrada after him.

Harold Godwinson was chosen as King by the Witan (the council of important earls and bishops) and crowned on 6th January 1066.

1.2 Preparations for the invasion

Harold spent the spring and summer of 1066 preparing for an invasion by William or Harald Hardrada.

- Harold remained in the south with his army, guarding the coast closest to France.

- Earls Edwin of Mercia and Morcar of Northumbria were left in the north with their army, to guard against a Viking invasion.

- By late summer, when there had been no sign of an invasion, the soldiers were keen to return home to gather their harvests.

William was also preparing for the invasion of England.

- First he had to convince his barons that the invasion was a good idea. Many wished to stay at home to look after their own lands.

- They were convinced by the promise of more lands in England and because William had managed to persuade Pope Alexander II to give his support.

- When William's fleet was gathered at Dives in late summer, the wind was blowing in the wrong direction. During September, William's army could only sit and wait for the wind to change.

Meanwhile, the wind was favourable for Harald Hardrada's army to sail from Norway.

- Hardrada's army defeated Edwin and Morcar at the Battle of Fulford on 20th September.

- He then went on to capture York and started pillaging the area.

- On hearing of the invasion, Harold decided to march his army north. They arrived to catch Hardrada by surprise, at Stamford Bridge near York.

✓ Try mapping out the events running up to the Battle of Stamford Bridge to help you remember them. Start with Harold being crowned king, then have three branches, one for each of Harold, William and Harald. You might start it like the chart below. You will need to add some more sub-branches to cover all the key points. Try and use pictures instead of words where you can.

For help with producing a chart like this, see *Study Skills*, pages 43–48.

Events leading to Battle of Stamford Bridge

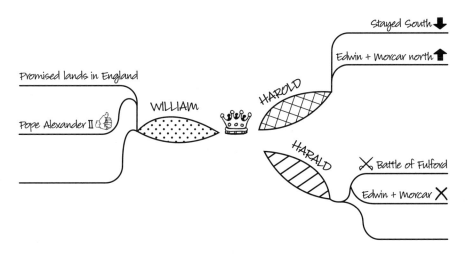

1.3 The Battle of Stamford Bridge, 25th September 1066

● As the English army approached, Hardrada led his army across a river to high ground. A small band of men was left to hold the bridge and delay the English for as long as possible.

● Hardrada formed his army into a shieldwall on the high ground.

● The archers and slingers in each army began by hurling missiles at each other.

● The English charged at the Vikings and were able to break up Hardrada's shieldwall.

● In the fighting, both Harald Hardrada and Tostig were killed.

Meanwhile, the wind had changed, allowing William's army to sail across the Channel.

● The Normans landed at Pevensey on 28th September. William's men were sent through the countryside, looting, burning and gathering food from the locals.

● Harold was still in the north when he found out about the Norman landing. His army was exhausted and many had been killed at Stamford Bridge.

● His brothers Leofwine and Gyrth advised him to rest and take time to build up a stronger force to fight the Normans. Harold, however, decided to march his army south straight away.

● Harold reached London on 6th October and continued south, while the Normans marched north from Pevensey to meet them.

1.4 The Battle of Hastings, 14th October 1066

The two armies met on the morning of 14th October, at a place outside Hastings called Senlac Hill.

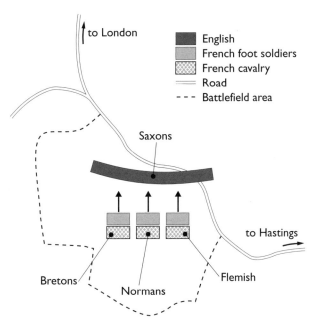

- The English formed a shieldwall along a ridge at the top of the hill.

- William's army formed three divisions in the valley below. The Bretons were on the left flank, Normans in the centre and Flemish on the right.

- The Norman archers began by firing into the English line. This had little effect as the English were well protected by their shields.

- Norman foot soldiers advanced up the hill to attack the English by hand, but they were unable to break the shieldwall.

- As the foot soldiers withdrew, the Norman knights advanced. Still the shieldwall held and the knights retreated.

- The Breton soldiers on the left flank of William's army decided to retreat hurriedly and ran back down the hill.

- When some of the ill-disciplined English fyrd broke ranks to follow the Normans down the hill, the knights regrouped and killed them.

- As the English shieldwall was weakened, Harold's brothers Leofwine and Gyrth were killed.

- In one final assault in the late afternoon, the Normans managed to collapse the shieldwall and reach the King's position. In the midst of the fighting, Harold was killed.

- At Harold's death, the remaining English army fled. William marched to London, gaining support on his way, and was crowned King on Christmas Day, 1066.

✓ Why William won the Battle of Hastings

Below is a flow chart showing why William won the Battle of Hastings rather than Harold. It summarises the key points, using abbreviated words and bubbles. To see how to produce a flow chart like this, see *Study Skills*, pages 49–53.

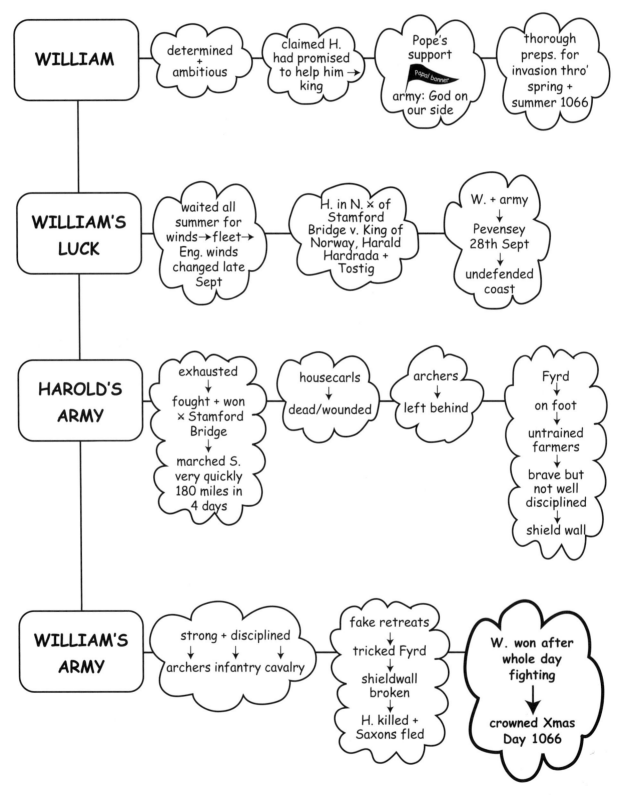

This flow chart was produced by Elizabeth Holtom and is taken from *Study Skills*, page 52.

Sample question

Try this sample essay question for yourself. A suggested answer is given at the back of the book.

Q.   (a) Describe the main events of the year 1066.   (20)

         (b) Explain the reasons why Harold lost the Battle of Hastings.   (10)

Summary

You should now know the following:

1.   The three main claimants to the crown of England in 1066.

2.   The preparations made by Harold and William before the invasion of England.

3.   The events of the Battle of Stamford Bridge.

4.   The events of the Battle of Hastings.

Test yourself

Before moving on to the next chapter, make sure you can answer the following questions. The answers are at the back of the book.

1.   According to William, what did Harold do in 1052 that entitled the Duke to the throne of England?

2.   Which member of Harold Godwinson's family supported Harald Hardrada?

3.   What was the Witan?

4.   When and where did the Normans land in England?

5.   When and where was the battle fought between Harold and William?

Chapter 2: Conquered England

William I needed to make sure that he could maintain control over the people, keeping them loyal to him and putting down any rebellions.

2.1 Medieval rule and the Feudal System

The Feudal System was a system of controlling the different levels of society and making sure that the King could raise an army when one was needed.

- The King owned all the land in the kingdom. He held some for himself to provide income for his household and government.

- The rest he gave to his tenants-in-chief, who were powerful barons and churchmen such as bishops. In return, the King expected them to be loyal to him.

- These tenants-in-chief demonstrated their loyalty by paying homage to the King. They knelt and solemnly swore fealty to him, becoming the King's vassal. They had to defend the King by providing soldiers from the lands they held.

- The tenants-in-chief gave some land to knights, who similarly paid homage to them and became their vassals.

- The knights also kept some land for themselves and gave the rest to freemen (or peasants), who made up the lowest level of the Feudal System.

KING

(Tenants-in-chief)

Bishop   Baron   Bishop   Baron

Knights   Knights   Knights   Knights

Freemen (Peasants)

2.2 Revolts and rebellions

William allowed some important Englishmen to keep their positions, as long as they swore fealty to him, but he soon regretted this decision.

● In 1069, the English earls Edwin of Mercia and Morcar of Northumbria rebelled with the help of some Vikings and Scots, taking the city of York.

● In revenge, William ordered that huge areas of Yorkshire be laid waste. This became known as the 'Harrying of the North'.

● Another English rebel, known as Hereward the Wake, operated in the marshlands of East Anglia. He has become a legendary figure with many stories told about him.

2.3 New buildings

In order to keep control over the people, the Normans introduced the castle to England.

● The first were motte and bailey castles. They were easy and quick to build, using local workers and materials. However, being wooden, they could be burnt down and would rot over time.

English people in important positions were gradually replaced by Normans. The new bishops began to rebuild churches in the Norman style, which typically used thick stone walls with rounded arches over the doors and windows.

2.4 The Domesday Book

The Domesday Book records the results of a nationwide survey ordered by William at Christmas 1085. Historians believe this was done for several reasons:

● A Viking invasion may have seemed likely. William wanted to know exactly how many soldiers he could recruit to defend his lands from the threat overseas.

● William may have suspected that some of his barons were holding land that should have belonged to him or the Church.

● William wanted to know where he could charge people more tax.

The Norman officials asked all the landholders for the following information:

● The name of the manor.

● The name of the landholder.

● The size of the land.

● How much belonged to the landholder.

● How many men worked on the land.

● How many amenities – such as mills or churches – were on the land.

● How much the land was worth.

> ✓ You could use pictures to help you remember the questions that were asked. Think what you would draw for each of the table entries below; the first one has been done for you.

Manor name	
Landholder name	
Land size	
Land held by landholder	
Number of men	
Amenities	
Value	

10

So that William could get an idea as to how things had changed over time, the questions were asked with reference to three periods:

- During the reign of King Edward (before 1066).

- When King William granted the land to the landholder (shortly after 1066).

- At the current time (around 1086).

2.5 Life in the manor

The manor was the unit of land used for farming.

- Freemen tended to be the wealthiest class of peasant. They generally governed the people who did the manual work.

- Villeins, or serfs, held their own land from the freemen and worked on it themselves.

- Cottars did not hold any land to farm themselves, but instead were hired to work on other people's land.

- Each village had a church and the most important manors also had a manor house where the lord of the manor lived.

The peasants in England used a system known as open-field farming.

- The land in a village consisted of two or three large, open fields. These would be divided into long strips of land, which were held by the freemen and villeins.

- The strips belonging to the lord of the manor formed his demesne. This would be ploughed each year, either by villeins or cottars.

- One of the fields would be left fallow during the year. It would be ploughed but no crop would be planted on it.

- There was also a meadow for growing long grasses that could be used as hay for the animals. Woodland provided wood for buildings and fuel. Common land was for people to graze their animals on.

- All the peasants in the village harvested the whole crop as one. The harvested corn was threshed and the grain was divided among all the farmers.

Sample question

Try this sample essay question for yourself. A suggested answer is given at the back of the book.

Q. (a) Describe the threats to his rule that William I faced. (20)

(b) Explain the steps that William took to gain control over the English people. (10)

Summary

You should now know the following:

1.   How the Feudal System worked.

2.   The main English revolts against William and how he dealt with them.

3.   The features of the new buildings the Normans introduced to England.

4.   The reasons for, and information contained within, the Domesday Book.

5.   The characteristics of an 11th-century manor.

Test yourself

Before moving on to the next chapter, make sure you can answer the following questions. The answers are at the back of the book.

1.   If a landholder swore fealty in an act of homage, what did he become?

2.   Which northern city did Edwin and Morcar re-take from the Normans?

3.   What were the typical features of Norman churches?

4.   What are the three periods of time referred to in the Domesday Book?

5.   Which class of peasant was paid wages to work because they did not hold land themselves?

6.   What was the name given to the land held by the lord of the manor?

Chapter 3: The sons of William I

William I had three sons: Robert, William and Henry.

On his deathbed, he declared that Robert would become the Duke of Normandy and William the King of England.

3.1 William II (1087–1100)

William II was known as 'Rufus' (the Red) and he ruled England for 13 years.

- He managed to crush rebellions, including one by his elder brother Robert, who believed that he should have been King of England.

- William believed that he ruled the Church in England, but Archbishop Anselm of Canterbury argued that the Pope was in charge. In 1097, Anselm left England in despair and William continued to take Church money and land.

- William II was killed in 1100; hit in the chest with an arrow while out hunting. His brother Henry quickly declared himself the new King of England.

3.2 Henry I (1100–1135)

Henry I was not a soldier, but he could be ruthless in getting what he wanted.

- Henry's brother Robert claimed once again to be the true King of England. The rebellion was put down and Robert was imprisoned for life.

- Henry's barons in France often started rebellions. All revolts were crushed, however, and Henry managed to hold on to Normandy.

- Henry encouraged monasteries to be built and appointed churchmen to important positions in government. He invited Anselm to return to England.

- But Henry and Anselm argued over who should appoint bishops and abbots. Anselm held his view that the Pope governed the whole Church. Henry felt that since these churchmen were often important government leaders and major landholders, he should choose them.

- A compromise was reached. The King would privately make his personal choice, then the Church would 'elect' this person officially.

3.3 Matilda

Henry had one legitimate son, named William, but in 1120 the young prince was drowned when his ship sank in the English Channel.

- Henry therefore wanted his daughter Matilda to become queen. His barons were very reluctant to agree because she was a woman.

- Henry arranged for Matilda to marry Geoffrey Plantagenet, hoping that Geoffrey would support her as queen.

- The barons were eventually persuaded to give Matilda their support.

- Geoffrey rebelled against the King and provoked Henry into fighting him in France. Henry died there in 1135.

☑ Use a flow chart to help you remember what happened to Robert, William II, Henry I and Matilda. The title could be 'What happened to William I's heirs' and then have four rows, one for each of Robert, William, Henry and Matilda. Summarise the key points for each in separate bubbles. The chart below shows how you might start it.

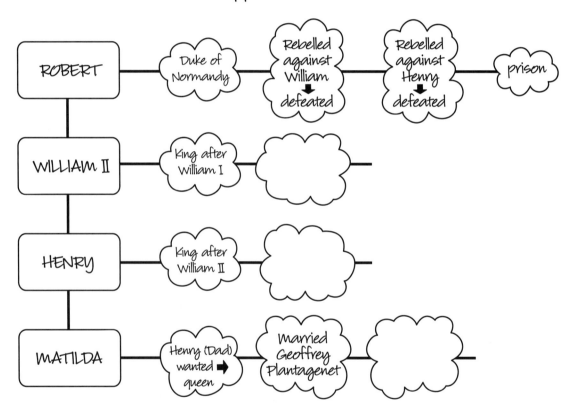

3.4 The Church

In the Middle Ages, the Church influenced every part of the life of every person.

● Priests preached that those who followed their religion would go to Heaven. Otherwise they would go to Hell. The people were reminded of Hell by murals painted on church walls.

● Mass was spoken in Latin, which only the educated could understand.

● The village priest would baptise babies, marry couples and bury the dead.

● A bishop was based in a cathedral. He was a significant landholder and was able to raise Church taxes called tithes.

● The bishops were controlled by the two archbishops of Canterbury and York. The Archbishop of Canterbury was the head of the Church in England.

● The head of the worldwide Church was the Pope, usually based in Rome.

3.5 Monasteries and nunneries

Some churchmen and women lived in monasteries and nunneries. Monks and nuns were supposed to follow the rules of their order, for example the order of St Benedict.

The three most important rules of St Benedict were:

● Obedience: following God's will, through the authority of the Church leaders.

● Poverty: not owning any earthly possessions.

● Chastity: not having relationships with the opposite sex, marrying or having children.

A typical day for a monk or a nun would be like this:

● Midnight: Matins, a church service lasting an hour.

● 6 am: Prime, another service, followed by breakfast and then work or study.

● 9 am: Chapter Mass, followed by a reading of the rules of the order in the Chapter House and a discussion on how the monastery should be run.

● 11 am: High Mass.

● Noon: Lunch, and an afternoon nap.

● 2 pm: Nones, another service, followed by work.

● 4 pm: Vespers, an evening service, followed by more work.

● 6 pm: Supper.

● 7 pm: Compline, the final service of the day, then bed.

✓ You could try using an index card to help you remember the typical day of a monk. Put the times on the front of the card and your answers on the back. To see how to produce index cards, see *Study Skills*, pages 54–58. Or, to remember the names of the services, why not try a mnemonic – try making up one of your own or use the one below.

Many **p**eople **c**hoose to **h**ave **l**unch;   Matins, Prime, Chapter, High, Lunch;

No one **v**olunteers for **s**upper **c**ompletely!   Nones, Vespers, Supper, Compline.

Monks and nuns often had a vital role to play in society.

- They provided education for youngsters who joined the order. Monasteries had large libraries full of books, which the monks would make copies of.

- Monasteries gave food to the poor and shelter to travellers. Often, local people would be employed as servants.

- If the monastery became too wealthy, the rules of St Benedict were sometimes forgotten and some monks began to live with more luxuries. Local people gave gifts of money because they believed that this would secure them a place in Heaven.

Sample question

Try this sample essay question for yourself. A suggested answer is given at the back of the book.

Q.   (a) Describe the typical day of a monk or nun in a monastery or nunnery.   (20)

   (b) Explain the effect that monasteries had on society and how society could affect them.   (10)

Summary

You should now know the following:

1.   The strengths and weaknesses of William II and the events of his reign.

2.   The strengths and weaknesses of Henry I and the events of his reign.

3.   The position of Henry's daughter Matilda.

4.   The features of the Church and its influence on the lives of ordinary people.

5.   The rules and daily life in the monasteries and nunneries.

Test yourself

Before moving on to the next chapter, make sure you can answer the following questions. The answers are at the back of the book.

1.   Which famous churchman quarrelled with William II?

2.   Why did Henry I face such a dilemma over who should succeed him?

3.   Why were church walls decorated with murals?

4.   How might increased wealth lead to a monastery not following the rules of St Benedict?

Chapter 4: From civil war to Henry II

4.1 Stephen (1135–1154)

When Henry died in 1135, Stephen, the Count of Blois, rushed to England and claimed the throne for himself.

- Stephen was the grandson of William the Conqueror.

- Henry's daughter, Matilda, sailed from France in 1139 and began to raise an army. However, when she marched on London, the people turned against her and Matilda was driven out of the city.

- The civil war lasted for 14 years. This period has become known as the Anarchy. The *Anglo-Saxon Chronicle* describes it as a period when '*Christ and his saints slept*'.

- Matilda left England in 1153 and her son Henry, the Duke of Normandy, continued the struggle on her behalf. He and Stephen agreed that Henry would take over the throne of England when Stephen died.

✓ You could make up a story that connects the facts of what happened once Henry I died, up until Henry II became King (see *Study Skills*, page 66). Ask someone to read the story back to you so that you can visualise the story unfolding in your head.

4.2 Henry II (1154–1189)

Henry II continued the work of his grandfather, Henry I, by increasing royal justice.

- He encouraged the growth of assizes. The assizes took power away from the barons' courts and this meant any fines obtained went directly to the King.

- Before the legal reforms, trials were often settled by ordeal.

4.3 Thomas Becket

Henry II's Royal Chancellor was Thomas Becket. Henry wanted Becket to take over when the Archbishop of Canterbury died, as he was keen to have an ally who would allow him to control the Church.

- Henry and Becket argued over the issue of criminous clerks. Henry wanted them to face trial in royal courts, meaning that any fines would come to the King.

- In 1164, the Constitutions of Clarendon stated that no one could be excommunicated without the King's permission; no churchman could leave England without the King's permission; and criminous clerks would be sentenced by the royal courts. Becket refused to accept these rules.

- Becket fled to France and Henry seized his lands. In the meantime, Henry decided to crown his son King of England in order that Henry could concentrate on his lands in France. When he attempted to use Archbishop Roger of York for the coronation, the Pope objected. Henry was forced to make peace with Becket in 1170.

- Becket excommunicated everyone who had been involved in the Prince's coronation. Outraged, the King is said to have shouted: '*Will no one rid me of this turbulent priest?*'

- On 29th December 1170, four knights rushed into Canterbury Cathedral and declared Becket a traitor. The knights set upon him with their swords and killed him.

- Henry was blamed for Becket's death. In penance, Henry prayed at Becket's tomb and walked through Canterbury allowing himself to be whipped.

✓ Try using a flow chart to show the rise and fall of Thomas Becket. Use pictures instead of words in the chart, for example the King and Becket arguing, Becket fleeing to France by boat, the knights killing Becket with their swords. It doesn't matter if you can't draw very well – use 'stick men' for the people and use different colours or captions to show who is who. The one below has been started for you.

Rise and fall of Thomas Becket

Sample question

Try this sample essay question for yourself. A suggested answer is given at the back of the book.

Q. (a) Describe the events that led to Henry II's falling-out with Thomas Becket. (20)

   (b) Which man – Henry or Thomas – do you think was more to blame for what happened? Explain your answer. (10)

4.4 Eleanor of Aquitaine and the sons of Henry II

Henry II's marriage to Eleanor of Aquitaine allowed the King to rule over most of France, and he spent most of his reign there.

Medieval France and the Angevin holdings

- Eleanor of Aquitaine had a strong and dominant personality. She had been married to King Louis VII of France, but the marriage was annulled in 1152 and Eleanor married Henry two months later.

- Henry and Eleanor had four sons: Henry, Richard, Geoffrey and John. The King often trusted Eleanor to look after his kingdom in England. Soon Eleanor began to side with her sons and against their father.

- The four brothers were impatient for power and quarrelled with their father. In 1173, encouraged by their mother, Princes Henry, Richard and Geoffrey rebelled against the King.

- Eleanor was imprisoned for the rest of the King's life. Henry spent two years trying to defeat the uprisings. Henry and Geoffrey died before their father, and Richard and John rebelled again in 1188 with the help of the King of France. Henry II died the following year.

Summary

You should now know the following:

1. The reasons for the civil war between Stephen and Matilda.

2. The work of Henry II in improving royal justice.

3. The struggle between the King and the Church that led to the murder of Thomas Becket.

4. The problems caused by Eleanor of Aquitaine and the four sons of Henry II.

Test yourself

Before moving on to the next chapter, make sure you can answer the following questions. The answers are at the back of the book.

1. Which three points of the Constitutions of Clarendon did Becket refuse to accept?

2. What event caused the Pope to object to Henry II's dealings with the Church?

3. Name four key people involved in the 1173 rebellion against Henry II.

Chapter 5: Richard I, the Crusades and King John

5.1 The First Crusade

The Crusades were a series of military expeditions to the Holy Land. They were launched with the intention of freeing Christian sites from Muslim control.

The Holy Land and the route of the First Crusade

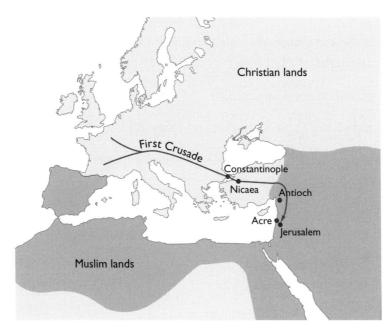

- Pope Urban II launched the First Crusade in 1095 to free the city of Jerusalem from the Muslims.

- Thousands of people made the 2,000-mile march to the Holy Land. However, they were undisciplined fighters and many were slaughtered by Muslim forces.

- A second wave of crusaders was led by nobles such as Robert of Normandy and Stephen of Blois.

- They managed to take the city of Antioch in June 1098. However, the Muslim army then surrounded the city, trapping the crusaders within the walls. They were forced to leave the city.

- The crusaders took Jerusalem a year later. The lands they controlled across the Holy Land were divided up into crusader states.

- The Second Crusade was launched in 1145 and was led by Louis VII of France – accompanied by his wife Eleanor of Aquitaine (see page 20). This army intended to reinforce the Christian soldiers in Jerusalem, but was forced to turn back in 1148 after a failed siege of the city of Damascus.

5.2 Richard I (1189–1199) and the Third Crusade

Richard I was devout, strong and courageous – earning the nickname 'Lionheart'. He travelled so much that he only spent six months of his ten-year reign in England.

- Richard and Philip II of France decided to lead a crusade in 1191.

- Richard arrived at Acre to find Philip's army of crusaders besieging the city, while surrounded by a Muslim army led by the commander Saladin. Acre eventually surrendered in July 1191 and a truce with Saladin was agreed.

- When the sick Philip returned to France, Richard was left in charge of the whole Crusade. He believed that Saladin was not keeping the agreed truce and ordered several thousand Muslim prisoners to be openly massacred in front of Saladin's army.

- The crusaders marched south, taking the city of Jaffa. Richard began to receive reports that his old ally Philip of France was preparing to take his French lands. Despite the best efforts of the crusaders, Saladin's forces still managed to hold Jerusalem.

- The Muslims then attempted to retake Jaffa from the crusaders. A stalemate was reached: with Saladin constantly attacking Jaffa, Richard was forced to defend the city and could not carry on to Jerusalem.

- The crusaders grew weary and ill, and eventually Saladin and Richard agreed a truce. Richard could keep all the land he had conquered down to Jaffa, but everything south of the city, including Jerusalem, had to be left for Saladin.

The route of the Third Crusade

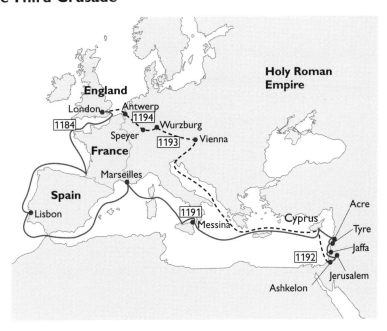

Richard left the Holy Land in October 1192. He soon found that many of his enemies had been plotting against him.

● Richard attempted to travel back through Austria and Germany. He was captured near Vienna and handed over to the Emperor of Germany, who demanded a ransom of 100,000 marks for his release. It took two years for the money to be raised, leaving England nearly bankrupt. Richard was set free in 1194.

● Philip of France had been plotting with Richard's brother John to take control of Normandy. Richard arrived in England and put down John's rebellion. He then spent the next four years in France fighting Philip, managing to reclaim most of the land that Philip had taken.

● In 1199, Richard was killed, almost by accident, when he was hit by a stray crossbow bolt. On his deathbed, Richard forgave his brother John and declared him to be his successor as King of England.

✓ Index cards could be a good way of remembering the sequence of events for the crusades. Use one card for each crusade. Think up questions for the fronts of the cards and write your answers on the back. For example, the card for the First Crusade might have the following questions on the front:

First wave:
Who?
When?
Where?
Second wave:
Who?
When?
Where?

Then test yourself by seeing if you can answer the questions.

Evidence question

You may be asked to answer an evidence question on Richard I. Refer to the guidance on pages xi–xii and make sure that you practise answering these questions.

5.3 John and the Angevin Empire

King John's holdings in France

John was known as 'Lackland' because, as his father's youngest son, he should not have inherited any land. As it turned out, he inherited both England and vast lands in France. But he was not very successful in keeping hold of it.

- Philip II of France now turned against John. He claimed that John's nephew Arthur – the son of his brother Geoffrey – had a better claim to the English throne and the Angevin lands (see the family tree on page 197). John captured and imprisoned his nephew, and agreed a treaty with him that made Philip respect his right to the throne.

- In 1200, John married Isabella of Angoulême, who had been betrothed to Hugh Lusignan. This annoyed the Lusignan family, who complained to Philip, who attacked John's French lands.

- John's nephew Arthur went missing in 1203, fuelling rumours that the King had had him murdered. John's mother Eleanor of Aquitaine died the following year. She had been well respected and after her death many barons refused to continue supporting her son. Normandy fell to Philip in 1204, followed by most of John's remaining land in France.

- John reintroduced a tax called scutage that was only supposed to be used in times of war.

5.4 John and the Church

John believed that he alone had the right to control the Church in England. When the Archbishop of Canterbury died in 1205, John wanted to choose his successor.

- Pope Innocent III nominated the scholar Stephen Langton to be the new Archbishop. When John refused to accept Langton, the Pope placed England under an interdict in 1208.

- John was excommunicated in 1209 but would still not give in. He only backed down in 1213, when the Pope started to encourage Philip II to invade England. This was too much of a risk for John to take. He agreed to accept Langton as Archbishop and swore fealty to the Pope.

5.5 Magna Carta

John now prepared to take his lands back from Philip II. But his plans fell apart and John was forced to agree a humiliating peace with the French King.

- This was the last straw for the nobles in England. When John refused to meet them to discuss matters, some barons raised an army against the King and marched to London in May 1215.

- John was forced to meet the rebel barons at Runnymede, near Windsor. There, the barons presented the King with the Magna Carta ('great charter'), listing their demands.

The Magna Carta was intended to restrict the powers of the King. Some of the 63 clauses still have consequences today:

- The King was to leave the Church to govern itself.

- The King could not raise taxes without the agreement of his nobles.

- The level at which the King could set certain taxes was restricted.

- Freemen were entitled to a fair trial and could not be fined, imprisoned or otherwise punished without one.

- Any punishment should be fair and fit the crime.

John had no intention of keeping his promises. He gathered together his few loyal barons and raised his own army.

- The rebel barons asked Philip II for help in their fight against John. The King of France sent soldiers over with his son, Prince Louis, whom the rebels declared the rightful King of England.

- In the civil war that followed, John had some successes but lost many of his treasures when trying to cross the Wash in East Anglia. He caught dysentery and died in October 1216.

✓ Try using a chart with different branches to help you remember what happened during John's reign. Start with John in the centre and have three branches – the Angevin Empire, the Church and the Magna Carta. Use pictures to sum up the key points and different colours for the different branches.

Evidence question

You may be asked to answer an evidence question on King John. Refer to the guidance on pages xi–xii and make sure that you practise answering these questions.

Summary

You should now know the following:

1. The reasons for, and events of, the First Crusade.

2. The events of the Third Crusade and the involvement of Richard I.

3. The circumstances surrounding the loss of John's French lands.

4. The reasons for the conflict between John and the Church.

5. The terms of the Magna Carta and the consequences of it.

Test yourself

Before moving on to the next chapter, make sure you can answer the following questions. The answers are at the back of the book.

1. Which city in the Holy Land did crusaders capture in 1098?

2. Describe the terms of the 1192 truce between Richard I and Saladin.

3. When was England placed under an interdict?

4. Where and when was the Magna Carta presented to the King?

Chapter 6: Henry III and the Edwards

6.1 Henry III (1216–1272)

Henry III became King on the death of his father John, when he was just nine years old.

- He inherited a country in turmoil, but some respected knights such as William the Marshal supported him. They convinced the rebel barons that Henry would not be like his father.

- Once the King had grown up, his barons were not as understanding. Henry appointed foreigners to his government, which angered them.

- Henry was a devout Christian. He rebuilt Westminster Abbey and agreed to go on a Crusade. Yet he annoyed the Pope by attempting to make his son the King of Sicily in 1238 and was threatened with excommunication.

- These two factors – the presence of foreigners in the government and the threat from the Pope – caused some of Henry's barons to rebel against him. Their leader was Simon de Montfort, the Earl of Leicester.

De Montfort and the rebels forced Henry and his son Edward to sign the Provisions of Oxford. The King agreed to listen to the views of his nobles in a Parliament, which was to be a meeting of the most important men in the country.

- However, Simon de Montfort was still not satisfied and continued to put pressure on the King to agree to more demands.

- The King and Prince Edward raised an army, but they were defeated at the Battle of Lewes in 1264. Both royals became de Montfort's prisoners.

- A plot was hatched to free Prince Edward, who escaped. The two sides met again at the Battle of Evesham in 1265.

- At the battle, the rebel army was completely destroyed, with de Montfort and all his closest followers killed.

Henry III had learned to respect the views of his barons. He began to use Parliament to advise him and help raise money.

> ✓ Use drawings to help you remember the events of the reign of Henry III. You could use a different drawing for each of the bullet points above or perhaps a couple of sketches containing all the different points.

6.2 Edward I (1272–1307)

By the time he came to the throne in 1272, Edward I had a reputation as a fine military leader.

- Edward tended to use Parliament to his benefit. He passed the Statute of Gloucester, which gave more power to the royal courts, and the Statute of Mortmain, which restricted the amount of land that could be given to the Church.

- However, Edward still believed that he could ignore Parliament's will on some matters. Knowing that a tax raise would need the approval of Parliament, he tried to raise money in other ways. For example, in 1290, he drove all the Jews out of England and confiscated their property.

6.3 Wales and Scotland

Edward I had an ambition to unite all parts of the British Isles under his leadership. He wanted the monarchs in Wales and Scotland to pay him homage.

The Welsh campaign

Wales at the time of Edward I

- Prince Llewelyn of Wales refused to pay homage to Edward. In retaliation, Edward sent three English armies into Wales in 1276–1277.

- The Welsh fought in mountainous areas such as Snowdonia. The English managed to cut them off from the island of Anglesey, where the Welsh obtained food supplies, and forced Llewelyn's men to surrender. Edward forced Llewelyn to pay him homage.

- Llewelyn and his brother David fought back in 1282, taking several English castles. Edward invaded Wales, using the same trick of cutting off Anglesey. Llewelyn was killed and David sentenced to be hanged, drawn and quartered as a traitor.

- Edward built a string of castles around the coastline that were stronger than any seen before (see pages 36–37). English law was introduced to Wales, and more and more English people began to settle there.

The Scottish campaign

- When Queen Margaret of Scotland died in 1290, she had no clear successor. The Scottish nobles nominated the three best candidates – John Baliol, Robert Bruce and John Hastings – and asked Edward to choose who should be king.

- Edward chose John Baliol, who was crowned King John of Scotland in 1292. But in 1295, John made an alliance with the King of France, who had seized Gascony from the English. Edward then invaded Scotland and took over John's kingdom.

- William Wallace gathered an army to fight against the English. He was victorious at the Battle of Stirling Bridge in 1297, but beaten at Falkirk the following year. He was eventually captured in 1305 and executed.

- Robert Bruce began to lead the Scottish rebels in 1306. Edward prepared another invasion of Scotland but died in northern England in 1307.

Evidence question

You may be asked to answer an evidence question on Edward I, Wales and Scotland. Refer to the guidance on pages xi–xii and make sure that you practise answering these questions.

6.4 Edward II (1307–1327)

The throne passed to Edward's son, also named Edward.

The Battle of Bannockburn, 24th June 1314

- Robert Bruce began to threaten the stronghold of Stirling Castle. Edward marched north with an army of 20,000 men.

- The two armies met at Bannockburn, south of Stirling Castle, on 23rd June 1314. The terrain forced the English into a tight wedge, with marshy land on both sides and a stream running between them and the Scots.

- One story claims that on the evening of 23rd June, an English knight named Henry de Bohun spotted Robert Bruce riding alone and charged with his lance. Bruce moved his horse to one side, raised his axe and brought it down through the knight's head.

- The next day, the English cavalry made several charges but could not break up the strong Scottish schiltrons. The English archers could only fire from the side of the field.

- This stalemate continued until the English spotted a crowd of people appearing to join the Scottish ranks from behind, which the English mistakenly believed to be armed reinforcements. Edward and his army retreated and fled.

6.5 The fall of Edward II

Edward depended on favourites to support his rule. These men were rewarded with important positions and land.

- The first of Edward's favourites was a French knight named Piers Gaveston. After his father's death, Edward II began to shower Gaveston with land and appointments.

- Edward left for France in 1308 and he appointed Gaveston to rule England while he was away, which angered many barons.

- Led by the Earl of Lancaster, and supported by Edward's wife, Queen Isabella, the barons forced Edward to have Gaveston exiled. When Gaveston returned to England, he was executed by Lancaster's men.

- After a while, the King began to find new favourites and gave huge amounts of land to Hugh Despenser and his son, also named Hugh.

- The barons rebelled in 1321 and once again forced Edward to send his favourites into exile. But this time, the King's army defeated the rebels the following year. Lancaster was executed and the Despensers returned to England. The Statute of York held that the King's power could not be challenged by his subjects.

- Queen Isabella hated Edward's favourites and began an affair with a rebel baron named Roger Mortimer. Together they plotted to overthrow the King.

- The whole of England turned against Edward II. The Despensers were executed and Edward was forced to abdicate in favour of his son, who became Edward III. He was imprisoned in Berkeley Castle where he was murdered in 1327.

✓ You could use a flow chart to plot what happened when Edward II became King until his murder in 1327. The first row of the chart could be the Battle of Bannockburn, the second row could be Piers Gaveston, the third Hugh Despenser, etc. Why not copy out the one below and add in the missing information.

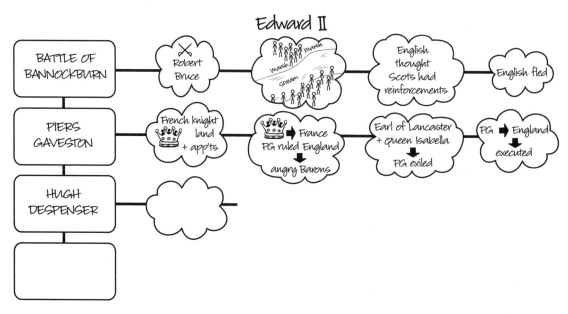

32

6.6 Edward III (1327–1377)

Edward III became King aged 15. When he was 17, he arrested his mother and her lover. Mortimer was executed for treason and Isabella was sent to a castle in Norfolk.

The Hundred Years' War

- Edward III decided to claim the throne of France, as he felt that he had a claim to the throne through his mother (see the family tree on page 198). However, the throne went instead to Philip of Valois, who became Philip VI.

- The French kings did not like the fact that the English controlled Gascony. They continued to give aid to the Scots in their rebellions.

The 1346 campaign

- In July 1346, Edward and 15,000 English soldiers sailed to Normandy. They headed east, looting and destroying the coastal towns.

- When they reached the River Seine, the English found that the French army had destroyed all the bridges. They were forced to march south-east towards Paris. At Poissy they managed to rebuild the bridge and cross safely.

- The French managed to reach the River Somme first and destroyed or guarded all the bridges. The English marched north-west and forced their way across the river at Blanchetaque, near Abbeville – straight into the path of Philip VI's army.

6.7 The Battle of Crécy, 26th August 1346

The two armies met in a field near the village of Crécy on the evening of 26th August 1346.

- The English army, made up of 12,000 foot soldiers, lined up on a ridge facing south-east. They stood in two large groups, commanded by the Earl of Northampton and Edward, Prince of Wales, nicknamed 'the Black Prince'. King Edward commanded a smaller group behind the main two.

- The French army, made up of between 30,000 and 40,000 men, stood in the valley below the ridge. They consisted mostly of mounted knights, with a long line of Genoese archers at the front.

- The English longbowmen fired constant barrages of arrows down onto the Genoese, who began to retreat.

- The French made several charges up to the ridge and at one point managed to reach Prince Edward's position. When a message reached King Edward that the Prince needed help, he dismissed it, saying that he wanted his son to 'earn his spurs'.

- Eventually the French horses and knights were exhausted and they retreated, having lost 10,000 men.

Edward then marched towards Calais, believing he could take the town easily.

- Calais was strongly fortified and Edward was forced to besiege the town. The siege lasted a year, but eventually the people of Calais surrendered.

- The French inhabitants were driven out of the city and replaced by English settlers.

6.8 The last years of Edward III

● The Black Death reached Europe in 1348, causing hostilities to pause for a few years. Edward was confident in placing command with his son, the 'Black Prince', who was largely successful in France.

● In England, there were protests about the heavy taxation needed to fund the war. Edward eventually allowed Parliament more control over taxation.

● In 1376, Parliament began to demand further reforms. In a session that became known as the Good Parliament, the barons demanded that the King's advisors be removed before any more money could be raised.

● By the following year, Edward's son John of Gaunt had used his strong influence to return many of the advisors to their positions.

Edward III died in 1377, having had four sons from his marriage to Philippa of Hainault (see the family trees on pages 198 and 199).

● The eldest son, 'the Black Prince', had died before his father, in 1376. On his deathbed, he had made his father and brother, John of Gaunt, swear that they would recognise his son Richard as the heir to the throne. At the time of the King's death the following year, Richard was just nine years old.

Summary

You should now know the following:

1.   The causes and events of the conflict between Henry III, Simon de Montfort and an emerging Parliament.

2.   The personality of Edward I and the events of his campaigns against Wales and Scotland.

3.   The details of the Battle of Bannockburn and the reasons for the overthrowing of Edward II.

4.   The events of the Hundred Years' War, including the 1346 campaign and the Battle of Crécy.

5.   The position of Edward III in England during his final years.

Test yourself

Before moving on to the next chapter, make sure you can answer the following questions. The answers are at the back of the book.

1.   At which battle was Simon de Montfort killed?

2.   Which trick did Edward I twice use to defeat Llewelyn of Wales?

3.   Who won the Battle of Stirling Bridge in 1297?

4.   Why did the English retreat hurriedly from the battlefield at Bannockburn?

5.   Which rebel baron plotted with Queen Isabella to overthrow Edward II?

Chapter 7: Life in the Middle Ages

7.1 Castles

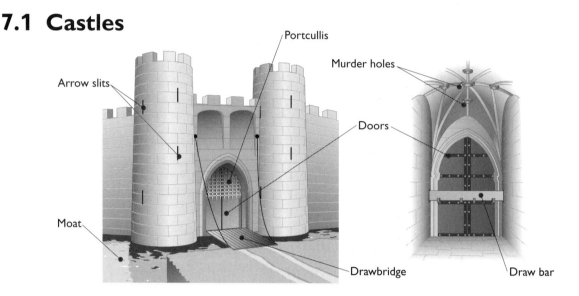

- The Normans brought the motte and bailey castle to Britain (see page 9). They could be constructed quickly, using local materials and labour. But being wooden, they could be burned and were susceptible to rot. Most did not last more than 20 years.

- Some motte and bailey castles were rebuilt as stone buildings. The wall around the bailey could become a curtain wall, and a shell keep or tower keep could be built on top of the motte to replace the wooden building.

- Medieval armies used siege warfare and the castles needed to withstand constant attempts to breach the walls. Many castles were surrounded by a moat. Over the moat was a drawbridge, which could be raised to prevent entry. In front of the main door was a portcullis, which could be dropped down, and a draw bar could be pulled across.

Hoardings: defences to protect the castle walls

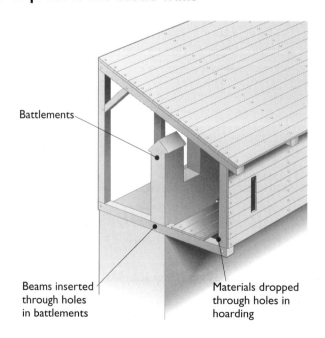

- In the ceiling behind the door, there were murder holes, through which boiling liquid could be poured. Wooden hoardings, built over the tops of the walls, also allowed defenders to fire downwards.

- One method of attack was to use a belfry, or siege tower, so that men could climb over the battlements. Another was to dig a tunnel underneath the wall, causing the wall to collapse. Defenders began to build round towers, which were stronger than square ones, and made the walls thicker at the bottom.

Trebuchet

Mangonel

Battering ram

- A battering ram could weaken a wall if there was no moat or slope. Stone-throwing machines, such as mangonels or trebuchets, had advantages as they could be used from a distance.

- The attackers could simply surround the castle and wait until the defenders' food and supplies ran out. Sometimes this could take months or even years.

- Edward I built a series of very strong castles in Wales (see page 30). These had a circle of defences surrounded by another and so are known as concentric castles.

Castles were also homes for rich nobles and their families, and the grandest ones were built to display the great wealth of the owner.

- There was usually a great hall, in which the family met and dined. The family slept in a smaller, private room called a solar. The most important people lived on the higher floors, and the servants and soldiers down below.

- A cellar held all the supplies, which were plentiful in case of a siege, and the castle had its own well to provide water.

- By the 1500s, people were building houses for comfort rather than defence. Castles began to be replaced by large country houses.

7.2 The Jews

- Jewish settlers in medieval Britain were mostly in the business of money lending. They were tolerated by kings and nobles, who often needed to borrow from them.

- Towards the end of the 12th century, Jews began to be subject to attacks called pogroms.

- The anti-Jewish feeling was stirred up by false stories about them. The stories, known today as blood libel, told of Jews kidnapping and murdering Christian children.

- By the 13th century, the government was passing anti-Jewish laws. Jews were not allowed to eat with Christians, or go out at Easter, and were made to wear yellow cloth in public. In 1275, they were banned from lending money, which deprived most Jews of their livelihood.

- In 1290, a law introduced by Edward I threw the Jews out of Britain altogether.

✓ Try using pictures to help you remember all the main points about Jews at the time. You could either put these in a table with the key words in the left-hand column and your pictures in the right-hand column, or draw a sketch which includes all the different elements. Think what other illustrations you could use for the table below.

Money lenders	£
Pogroms	
Blood libel	
Anti-Jewish laws	
Out of Britain	

7.3 Medieval women

- In the Middle Ages, women were expected to work as hard as the men. They had to help their husbands work in the fields, cutting hay and corn and looking after the animals, and had to make produce such as cheese and butter, and then sell it at market. Some women took on extra work brewing ale or baking bread. They were expected to declare to their husbands any extra income they earned.

- Some women ran successful businesses in their own right. An example is Margery Kempe, who made a fortune brewing ale in King's Lynn, Norfolk. Another educated woman, also from Norfolk, was Margaret Paston, who was forced to take care of her husband's business while he was away.

- Upper-class women whose husbands held powerful positions were sometimes able to influence history in important ways. We know of Matilda, whose struggle to be recognised as queen caused a civil war with her cousin, and Eleanor of Aquitaine and Isabella of France, who both contributed significantly to the downfall of their husbands.

Evidence question

You may be asked to answer an evidence question on women in medieval society. Refer to the guidance on pages xi–xii and make sure that you practise answering these questions.

7.4 Medieval health and the Black Death

Doctors in the Middle Ages relied on the works of ancient Greek and Roman doctors, such as Galen, whose writings were largely out of date.

- Remedies for illnesses were based on superstition and were often dangerous. Patients were cut and left to bleed in the hope that the infection would escape. Later on, leeches were used to suck the blood from the body.

- It was believed that diseases were carried by smells in the air and were a punishment from God for disobedience.

- These false beliefs meant that proper prevention was impossible. Towns had poor sanitation, with no running water or drainage. The average person only lived for 40 years, with most deaths occurring during childhood. Childbirth often resulted in the mother's death.

The Black Death, a disease that originated in Asia, spread throughout Europe and reached Britain in 1348.

- Bubonic plague (*Yersinia pestis*) caused a bubo – a large swollen lymph gland – to appear in the armpit or groin. The victim usually died within five days.

- The plague arrived in Britain in June 1348, carried on two ships which landed at Melcombe in Dorset.

- Despite various attempts to stop the advance of disease, the people were powerless. The sick were abandoned and city gates were closed to strangers who might have brought the plague inside the walls. Flowers and herbs were used to purify the air and fires were lit.

- The Black Death affected the Church terribly. Priests caught the disease themselves through contact with the sick. A group of people called flagellants, who believed that by whipping themselves they could persuade God to lift the punishment, were unsuccessful.

> ✓ Make up a story that describes the spread of the Black Death, how it affected the people of Britain and what people did to try to stop it. Imagine the story in your head: see it as a film being played back as you think of the people who died and the flagellants whipping themselves to try to rid the country of the disease.

It is believed that at least a third of England's population was wiped out by the Black Death. As a result, the country lacked workers and resources.

- Surviving workers found themselves in demand and the lords who employed them had to pay much more for their services. Parliament passed the Statute of Labourers in 1351, which stated that all peasants had to work at the same rate as they had done in 1348. But many lords were forced to provide better working conditions and pay higher wages. The price of food increased because it was costing more to produce.

> *Evidence question*
>
> You may be asked to answer an evidence question on the Black Death. Refer to the guidance on pages xi–xii and make sure that you practise answering these questions.

Summary

You should now know the following:

1.   The layout and facilities of a typical medieval castle.

2.   The position of Jews during the Middle Ages.

3.   The position of women during the Middle Ages.

4.   The causes, events and consequences of the Black Death in Britain.

Test yourself

Before moving on to the next chapter, make sure you can answer the following questions. The answers are at the back of the book.

1.   What was the notable design feature of Edward I's castles in Wales?

2.   What is the name for an anti-Jewish attack?

3.   Which Norfolk woman handled her husband's business during his absence?

4.   What is the name of the bacteria that causes bubonic plague?

5.   Who were flagellants and what did they attempt to do?

Chapter 8: Richard II and life in the towns

8.1 Richard II (1377–1399) and the Peasants' Revolt

His father having died the year before, Richard II inherited the throne in 1377 from his grandfather Edward III. He was placed into the care of his powerful uncle, John of Gaunt.

- Richard faced a serious crisis in 1381, when the villeins began to cause unrest in the countryside.

- The government introduced a Poll Tax in 1377. This was again raised in 1379 and in 1381, when it was trebled to one shilling, payable by everyone over the age of 14. It was almost impossible for peasants to afford this and they rose up against the government agents who had been sent to collect the money.

- The uprising spread throughout the south-east of England. Rebel leaders appeared, such as Wat Tyler in Kent. In June 1381, the rebels marched on London and demanded to speak to the King.

- Richard agreed to meet the rebels at Mile End on 14th June. He promised that people would in future be fairly paid and that nobody would be punished for the revolt. However, some of the rebels managed to break into the Tower of London and execute the Archbishop of Canterbury and the King's Treasurer.

- Richard again agreed to meet the rebels at Smithfield on 15th June. A supporter of the King insulted Wat Tyler and in the scuffle that followed the rebel leader was killed.

- Richard took control, calling out to the rebels that he was their true leader, and telling them to go home. Richard did not keep his promises and the other rebel leaders were captured and executed.

✓ A flow chart could be a useful tool to help you remember the sequence of events of the Peasants' Revolt. Pick out the key words from each bullet point and, where possible, use pictures in your bubbles for these words.

Sample question

Try this sample essay question for yourself. A suggested answer is given at the back of the book.

Q. (a) Describe the events of the Peasants' Revolt in 1381. (20)

(b) Explain the reasons why the peasants marched on London. (10)

8.2 The fall of Richard II

Richard II had handled the Peasants' Revolt well but soon became over-confident. He resented being under the control of his uncle John of Gaunt and tried to force Parliament to increase his powers.

● Parliament resisted, and in the Merciless Parliament of 1388, the nobles demanded the arrest of Richard's supporters. The Lords Appellant took control of the government away from the King.

● In 1389, power was returned to Richard, who took several steps to increase his authority. He formed a permanent guard of personal knights and increased taxes, without the approval of Parliament.

● In 1397, Richard took his revenge on the Lords Appellant. One was executed, another murdered and the other three were sent into exile. One of these exiled lords was Henry Bolingbroke, the son of Richard's uncle, John of Gaunt.

● In February 1399, John of Gaunt died and Richard seized his uncle's lands instead of allowing them to go to Henry Bolingbroke. Bolingbroke came to England in June, gathered support from the nobles and arrested the King.

● Richard was deposed by Parliament in September 1399 and imprisoned in the Tower of London. Bolingbroke was crowned King Henry IV the following month. Richard was taken to Pontefract Castle, where he was murdered in February 1400.

8.3 Towns

While most people still lived in the countryside, the medieval period saw great growth in towns.

The structure of a medieval town house

- Buildings were made from a timber frame, with walls made with wattle and daub. The roofs were either thatched with straw or tiled.

- The streets were laid out so that there were several areas of common land for animals to graze and a large open area which was used as a marketplace for traders.

- Nearby would be a church or churches, and often a monastery or nunnery.

- Towns housed large groups of beggars, who targeted the wealthy tradesmen who lived in the towns to be close to their businesses.

- Boys who wanted to learn a trade for themselves first became apprentices, who were attached to a master craftsman by an agreement called an indenture. The master craftsmen taught them their trade and had to feed and clothe them. He would receive their labour and a sum of money from their families in return. Once the apprentices finished their training, they became journeymen and were able to work for their own wages.

8.4 Guilds

The tradesmen and craftsmen of a town sometimes formed an organisation together called a **guild**.

The idea of a guild was that the tradesmen and craftsmen would work together to protect each other's trade.

- Each guild had its own rules regarding who could set up business in their trade, the quality of the goods traded and the number of apprentices to be trained.

- Dishonest tradesmen who broke the rules of the guild were punished, usually by humiliation in front of the town. The usual way of doing this was to place the accused in a pillory or the stocks.

- The most important guildsmen had the chance to become mayor of the town and represent all the citizens. The wealthiest guilds were able to build guildhalls in which to meet.

- Guilds also put on town events such as pageants, mystery plays for entertainment and miracle plays, which had a religious message.

8.5 Town government, law and order

- Towns began to be granted charters by their lord or the King, which allowed the townspeople to form their own town government, and produce some of their own laws and taxes.

- There were no police, but watchmen kept a lookout for criminals. If one was seen, a great shout went up (called the 'hue and cry') and anyone who heard it was obliged to chase after the criminal.

- The town governments had to deal with all the waste and rubbish produced every day. A channel was set into the middle of the road for foul water to drain away.

- Fire could be a real hazard in towns. Businesses that needed open fires were often sited away from the centre of town to reduce the risk.

Summary

You should now know the following:

1. The causes and events of the Peasants' Revolt of 1381.

2. The reasons for the downfall of Richard II.

3. The typical businesses and people found in a medieval town.

4. The position of guilds in medieval towns.

5. The issues relating to town government and law and order.

Test yourself

Before moving on to the next chapter, make sure you can answer the following questions. The answers are at the back of the book.

1. In which three years was the Poll Tax raised?

2. How did Richard II deal with the Lords Appellant in 1397?

3. By which agreement was an apprentice held in the service of a master craftsman?

4. What was needed for a town to appoint its own government?

Chapter 9: The three Henrys

9.1 Henry IV (1399–1413)

Though Parliament had supported Henry IV, he had deposed his cousin Richard II illegally. Furthermore, his cousin the Earl of March had a better claim to the throne. The first few years of his reign were full of troubles.

- A Welshman named Owain Glyndwr claimed to be the true Prince of Wales. He and his followers captured many of the important castles in Wales that had been built by Edward I.

- There was an attempt to replace Henry with the Earl of March in 1403. The rebels joined with Owain Glyndwr and met the King and his son Henry, Prince of Wales, at Shrewsbury on 21st July 1403. In the ensuing battle the rebels were soundly defeated.

- The Scots attempted a rebellion but were swiftly crushed. The French tried to reclaim the English lands in Calais and Gascony, but these attempts also failed.

Henry IV was also notable for his reasonably good relations with Parliament.

- The constant threats to his rule led to expensive military campaigns and Henry faced money problems throughout his reign. However, he was willing to co-operate with Parliament, whose members were mostly supportive of him.

- Parliament appointed royal councillors to help with the King's finances. When Henry's health started to fail him, these men, together with his son Henry, took on more of the King's responsibilities.

> ✓ You could use index cards to help you remember the main events of Henry IV's reign. Think up suitable questions for the front of the card, with your answers on the back. Then add other cards for Henry V and Henry VI.

9.2 Henry V (1413–1422)

Henry V came to the throne with a great deal of military experience. He also kept a tight hold on his finances and strongly supported the Church. But Henry is best known for his campaigns to claim land in France.

- Henry was helped by the fact that France was in the middle of a civil war. The Burgundians and the Armagnacs were fighting each other to gain the throne, and both tried to entice Henry on to their side.

- In August 1415, Henry and his army landed in Normandy. His tactic was to progress deep into France with a *chevauchée* (a fast hit-and-run raid).

- The defences at Harfleur were strong and the town did not fall until September. Meanwhile, dysentery had spread through the English ranks and the *chevauchée* had to be abandoned.

- Instead, the English marched north-east along the coast towards Calais. The Armagnacs and Burgundians joined forces to intercept them.

- On 24th October, the English found their path blocked from the north. Some sources wrote that there were as many as 60,000 French soldiers against a force of only 6,000 Englishmen. The two sides took up their positions and waited overnight, just outside the town of Agincourt.

9.3 The Battle of Agincourt, 25th October 1415

- The English lined up in three ranks, with Lord Camoys commanding the group on the left, Henry in the centre and the Duke of York on the right.

- The battlefield lay in a plain with woods on either side, forcing the two armies into a narrow field of combat. The French arranged themselves in three ranks, one behind the other, and simply waited for reinforcements to arrive.

- Henry gave the order for the English to close in on the enemy. The archers planted stakes in the ground to protect them from the French cavalry. The two sides were now only 300 yards apart.

- As the first line of French foot soldiers advanced, the English archers were forced to drop their bows and fight hand to hand. The muddy field hindered the French infantry with their heavy plate armour, and once on the ground it was difficult for them to get up again.

- The second line of French soldiers now had to clamber over piles of bodies to reach the English and the French line gradually fell apart.

- Any French knights still alive were captured and taken to the rear of the English line, to be held for ransom. When a rumour spread that the English were under attack from behind, Henry rashly ordered all the prisoners to be killed.

- The third and final French line retreated. The battle had lasted four hours and Henry had won an incredible victory, having lost as few as 300 men. In contrast, the French lost around 10,000 men in total.

The Battle of Agincourt

While he is best known for his victory at Agincourt, Henry later returned to France and achieved even more success.

- In 1417, Henry captured all of the most important towns in Normandy. Once again, he was helped by the fact the Burgundians and Armagnacs had renewed their civil war.

- Henry helped the Burgundian forces to surround Paris and capture King Charles VI of France. In return, a marriage was arranged between Henry and the King's daughter, and Henry was named as heir to the French throne.

- Campaigning in France in 1422, Henry fell ill with dysentery and died. He left a nine-month-old son, also named Henry, as King of England and France.

- Until 1437, when he turned 16, Henry VI was a King in name only. His realm was governed for him by his two uncles: the Duke of Gloucester, who was in charge of England, and the Duke of Bedford, who controlled the fortunes of the English in France.

Sample question

Try this sample essay question for yourself. A suggested answer is given at the back of the book.

Q.   (a) Describe the events of Henry V's French campaign of 1415, up to just before
        the Battle of Agincourt.   (20)

       (b) Explain why Henry V was successful at Agincourt.   (10)

47

9.4 Joan of Arc

- As a young girl, Joan of Arc believed that she heard messages from God, telling her to save France from the English. In 1428, when she was around 16 years old, she was taken to see the Dauphin, the son of Charles VI.

- The Dauphin told her to help save the city of Orléans, which had been held under siege by the English for months.

- The siege collapsed and the English were driven away. The French continued on to other English strongholds and freed them. Joan gained a reputation for being invincible.

- Eventually, they liberated the city of Reims, which was the traditional place for French kings to be crowned. When the Dauphin became King Charles VII, Joan was given a prominent place at the coronation.

- However, Joan's forces failed to liberate Paris and she was wounded. Eventually, she was captured and handed over to the English, who imprisoned her at Rouen.

- The English accused Joan of being a witch. In a largely unfair trial, she was found guilty of witchcraft and was sentenced to be burnt at the stake on 30th May 1431, when she was just 19 years old.

> ✓ To help you remember all the key points of Joan of Arc's life, use a chart to map these out. Perhaps use the following words for the branches: 'Who', to describe the sort of person she was; 'Battles', to list the key cities she helped or failed to liberate; 'Capture', to describe the events leading to her death. You could use the one below as a starting point. Try thinking of some pictures to use instead of the words.

Joan of Arc

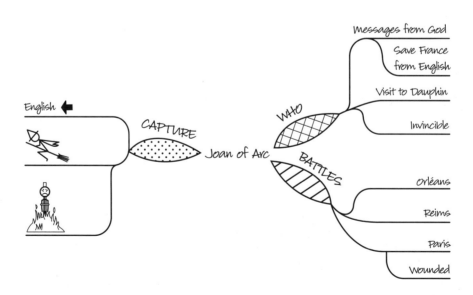

9.5 Henry VI (1422–1471)

Henry VI was finally able to rule his kingdom in 1437. He appeared intelligent and handsome, but was not a natural soldier and did not seem interested in warfare.

- Henry negotiated a truce with France and married Margaret of Anjou, a French noblewoman. Seeing Henry as a weak king, the French seized most of the land that had been lost to the English.

- This was partly the reason for a rebellion in Kent in 1450, led by Jack Cade. The rebels confronted the King in July, demanding that his government be reformed and his councillors replaced.

- After three days, the people of London forced the rebels back over London Bridge and drove them out of the city. Cade was wounded and died before he could face trial.

At this point, Henry's heir was Richard, Duke of York. But Richard had powerful enemies at court who were determined not to let him come to power.

- Queen Margaret had been accused of plotting with the Duke of Suffolk to prevent Henry dealing with Parliament and the Duke of York. After Suffolk's murder, the Duke of Somerset, rather than York, became Henry's closest advisor.

- The situation in France slowly began to improve, with some towns returned to English control. Parliament worked well with the King and agreed to raise taxes.

- But in the summer of 1453, the King suffered a mental collapse and was unable to carry out his duties.

9.6 The coming of civil war

- Richard, Duke of York, became Protector. The Duke of Somerset was arrested and placed in the Tower of London.

- In 1455, the King appeared to recover. York was dismissed and Somerset was freed, becoming Henry's advisor once more. York's supporters feared that they would be arrested.

- York's supporters are termed 'Yorkists' because they supported the Duke of York descended from Edmund of York, the son of Edward III. King Henry's supporters are termed 'Lancastrians' because Henry was descended from John of Gaunt, the Duke of Lancaster, also a son of Edward III (see the family tree on page 199).

- The Yorkists, led by Richard, gathered an army and marched south. On 22nd May 1455, they met a Lancastrian army, led by Henry and the Duke of Somerset, at St Albans.

- In the ensuing battle, the Duke of Somerset was killed. Henry VI was captured and forced to restore the Duke of York to his old position of Protector.

Summary

You should now know the following:

1.   The notable events in the reign of Henry IV.

2.   The events of Henry V's 1415 French campaign.

3.   The events of the Battle of Agincourt and its consequences for England and France.

4.   The life and deeds of Joan of Arc, and her demise.

5.   The early events of Henry VI's reign.

6.   The power struggles that led to civil war (the Wars of the Roses).

Test yourself

Before moving on to the next chapter, make sure you can answer the following questions. The answers are at the back of the book.

1.   Which Welsh rebel fought at the Battle of Shrewsbury in 1403?

2.   What was the name for a swift hit-and-run attack, used by Henry V in France?

3.   What was the charge against Joan of Arc that allowed the English to execute her?

4.   Who led the Kentish rebellion of 1450?

Chapter 10: The Wars of the Roses

10.1 The first war (1459–1461)

The Wars of the Roses

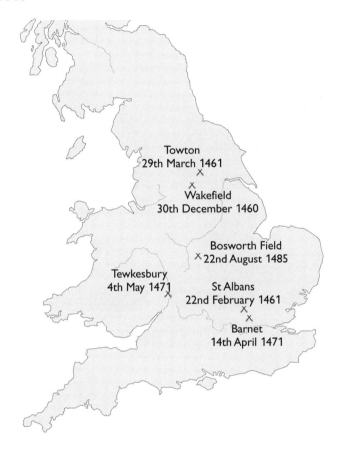

The Wars of the Roses are named after the emblems used by the Yorkists and Lancastrians. Richard of York's emblem was the white rose, while the Lancastrians used the red rose.

- In 1459, Queen Margaret declared Richard of York and his supporters to be traitors. Effectively, she was calling for them to be executed.

- The Yorkists seized London and captured Henry VI. Henry and Richard agreed to sign the Act of Accord on 25th October 1460. This declared that Richard would become King on Henry's death.

- An unhappy Margaret gathered a force of Lancastrians in the north. They met the Yorkists at the Battle of Wakefield on 30th December 1460 and Richard of York was killed.

- The Lancastrians defeated another Yorkist force led by Richard Neville, the Earl of Warwick, at St Albans on 22nd February 1461, and Henry VI was freed.

- But then the Lancastrians were refused entry into London. Richard of York's son Edward was marching from the West Country with more Yorkists. Fearing this large force, the Lancastrians withdrew, and the Yorkists were allowed into the city.

- The new head of the Yorkists was crowned King Edward IV by his followers. He then led his army in pursuit of the Lancastrians. The two sides met at Towton, in Yorkshire, on 29th March 1461.

- The resulting battle was the largest and bloodiest ever fought in Britain. It is believed that more than 8,000 Lancastrians and 5,000 Yorkists died on that day. Henry VI, Queen Margaret and Prince Edward fled to Scotland. The Yorkist Edward IV was now King of England.

The Wars of the Roses (part one)

1459 Margaret, wife of Henry VI, declares Richard, Duke of York a traitor.

Richard of York and his followers seize London and capture Henry VI.

25 Oct 1460 Act of Accord: Henry to remain as King. Richard of York to be King after him.

30 Dec 1460 Battle of Wakefield: Margaret defeats and kills Richard of York.

22 Feb 1461 Battle of St Albans: Margaret defeats Richard Neville, Earl of Warwick and recaptures Henry VI.

Margaret marches to London but is refused entry.

Edward, son of Richard of York claims the throne and joins with Richard Neville of Warwick.

29 Mar 1461 Battle of Towton: Edward son of Richard of York and Richard Neville of Warwick defeat Margaret.

10.2 Edward IV (1461–1483)

Edward IV had put the Lancastrian army to flight but his opponents still had many important nobles on their side. The new King therefore could only depend on a few important Yorkist figures. One of these was Richard Neville, the Earl of Warwick.

- Warwick is often known as the 'Kingmaker', because his support was important for a successful claim to the throne.

- However, Warwick soon fell out with Edward. He was annoyed when the King married Elizabeth Woodville, from a rival family who Warwick felt were gaining too much influence.

- Warwick plotted with Edward's brother George, Duke of Clarence, to remove the King from the throne. In 1469, the pair invaded from Calais, but they did not receive support from other nobles and fled back to France.

- Warwick decided to ally with the Lancastrians. Joined by Henry VI and Queen Margaret, he invaded England again in 1470. This time Edward fled the country and Henry VI was back on the throne.

10.3 The second war (1470–1471)

- While abroad, Edward was reconciled with his brother George, Duke of Clarence. The brothers raised an army and invaded. At Barnet, north of London, on 14th April 1471, the Lancastrians were defeated and Warwick was killed.

- The Yorkist army met the Lancastrians at the Battle of Tewkesbury on 4th May 1471 and Henry VI's son Prince Edward was killed. Henry was placed in the Tower of London, where he died on 21st May 1471.

- Edward IV's position as King was finally secure. He was generous to his nobles and his own brother Richard, Duke of Gloucester, became extremely powerful and had a lot of influence at court.

- Edward IV died on 9th April 1483, expecting his 12-year-old son to be crowned Edward V.

The Wars of the Roses (part two)

Edward, son of Richard of York, is now King Edward IV supported by Richard Neville of Warwick, known as 'The Kingmaker'.

1464 Edward IV secretly marries Elizabeth Woodville.

1469 Warwick 'The Kingmaker' joins Edward IV's brother George, Duke of Clarence and invades England.

1470 Edward IV drives Warwick out of the country.

Warwick joins up with Queen Margaret and Henry VI, and invades again.

Edward IV is forced to flee the country.

1471 Edward IV joins with his brother George of Clarence.

14 Apr 1471 Battle of Barnet: Edward IV and George of Clarence defeat and kill Warwick.

4 May 1471 Battle of Tewkesbury: Edward IV defeats Queen Margaret and kills Prince Edward.

21 May 1471 Mad old King Henry VI dies in the Tower of London. Edward IV is safely king again.

Edward's brother Richard, Duke of Gloucester becomes very powerful.

1478 Edward's other brother George of Clarence is executed for treason, drowned, according to some, in a barrel of wine.

9 April 1483 Edward IV dies leaving a 12-year-old son, Edward V as King.

10.4 Edward V and Richard III (1483–1485)

On his father's death, the young King Edward V found himself in the middle of a power struggle. His mother's family, the Woodvilles, battled with his father's brother Richard, Duke of Gloucester, to control him.

- Richard used his position to have his opponents executed. King Edward and his younger brother Prince Richard were placed in the Tower of London, supposedly for their own safekeeping.

- In July 1483, his uncle declared that the marriage of Edward IV and Elizabeth Woodville had been invalid. Therefore the two brothers were illegitimate and Edward was not the rightful King.

- Instead, Richard argued, as the next in line to the throne, *he* should be crowned King Richard III. This was done on 6th July 1483 and the two 'Princes in the Tower' were never seen again.

- Nobody is quite sure what happened to the two boys, but most historians agree that they were murdered in the Tower, and probably by men working on the orders of Richard III.

Richard III had a short and unsettled reign. He was popular among the northern nobles, but viewed with suspicion in the south. By the end of 1483, there were rumours circulating about the fate of the Princes in the Tower and the King's involvement.

- In November 1483, there was a revolt against Richard by an important ally, the Duke of Buckingham, which the King managed to put down. The following year, Richard's son and wife both died, leaving him without an heir.

- The main threat to his rule came from the Earl of Richmond, Henry Tudor, who had a weak claim to the throne. Henry had supported Buckingham in the 1483 revolt but had escaped to France.

- With French support, Henry sailed to Wales in August 1485 and gathered an army. They met Richard's forces on 22nd August, outside the town of Market Bosworth in Leicestershire.

10.5 The Battle of Bosworth, 22nd August 1485

- The armies took up their positions: Richard's on the top of Ambion Hill; Henry's near the marshes below. For the Yorkists, the Duke of Norfolk commanded the front rank and the Earl of Northumberland the rear. Henry's smaller army was led by the Earl of Oxford.

- Lord Thomas Stanley and Sir William Stanley had been supporters of the King. Richard hoped that they would stay loyal and fight for him. At Bosworth, the Stanleys' armies stood to one side to see what would happen.

- Norfolk led his forces down the hill to meet Oxford's ranks. In the vicious hand-to-hand fighting, Norfolk was killed.

The Battle of Bosworth

- Henry rode towards the Stanleys, appealing for them to join him. Seeing Henry now unprotected, Richard led his close guard in a cavalry charge across the battlefield.

- The Stanleys saw the threat to Henry and at this moment decided to join his side. They intercepted Richard before he could reach his target.

- Meanwhile, Richard's rear division, led by the Earl of Northumberland, watched the King's downfall from the top of Ambion Hill. It seems that they too had decided to support Henry.

- Richard's horse was killed underneath him and he was cut down trying to fight back on foot.

- At the death of Richard III, the Yorkist armies rode off. Richard's crown was retrieved by Lord Stanley and placed on the head of Henry Tudor, who was now declared King Henry VII.

Sample question

Try this sample essay question for yourself. A suggested answer is given at the back of the book.

Q.　(a) Describe the events that led to Edward IV gaining the throne in 1461.　(20)

　　　(b) Explain why Henry VI was able to regain the throne in 1470.　(10)

Summary

You should now know the following:

1.   The causes and events of the First War of the Roses (1459–1461).

2.   The notable events of the reign of Edward VI.

3.   The causes and events of the Second War of the Roses (1470–1471).

4.   The possible fate of Edward V and his brother Richard (the 'Princes in the Tower').

5.   The threats to the reign of Richard III.

6.   The events and outcome of the Battle of Bosworth.

Test yourself

Before moving on to the next chapter, make sure you can answer the following questions. The answers are at the back of the book.

1.   What were the two symbols of the Yorkists and the Lancastrians?

2.   By which nickname is Richard Neville, Earl of Warwick, often known?

3.   At which battle was Henry VI's son Edward killed?

4.   On what grounds did Richard III claim that Edward V was not the rightful King?

5.   Which Yorkist commander failed to come to the aid of Richard III at the Battle of Bosworth?

Part B: The Making of the United Kingdom: 1485–1750

Chapter 11: Henry VII (1485–1509)

11.1 Securing the throne

Henry was unprepared to become King. He had no experience of government and had been in exile for many years. He used several methods to hold on to his throne.

Uniting the country

- Henry knew that a country divided by war was not stable. He therefore took steps to unite the two sides.

- Henry married his cousin Elizabeth of York, the daughter of Edward IV and sister of Edward V. This was done both to unite the houses of Lancaster and York, and to satisfy anyone who felt that the throne should have passed to Elizabeth on the death of her uncle, Richard III.

Controlling the nobility

- Henry needed a nobility that was strong enough to support him, but not strong enough to turn against him. Many nobles had been killed in the Wars of the Roses. Henry replaced them with educated men from lower classes who served him in government.

- Yorkists were stripped of their titles and had their lands confiscated. Lancastrians who had been deprived of their lands by Edward IV had them restored.

- The Court of Star Chamber dealt with any rebellion among the nobility. Punishments included fines and the further confiscation of land from traitors.

- Justices of the Peace were appointed to help maintain law and order, and keep the court system working.

Retaining

- Retaining was the practice of holding a personal army. Henry believed it was potentially dangerous for nobles to keep private armies, which might instead be used against him.

- The Law of Livery restricted the number of soldiers that lords were allowed to keep. They also had to sign a recognisance, whereby they agreed to forfeit a large sum of money if they acted disloyally.

The Council

- Henry began to take away the nobles' right to attend his Council, which started to become full of educated men who were serving the King's government, such as Richard Empson, Edmund Dudley, Edward Poynings and Reginald Bray.

- Men like these were appointed to run the Court of Star Chamber and the Court of Requests. There was also a court set up to control retaining.

- Henry also set up the Council of Wales and re-started the Council of the North. This was to extend his power into areas where he had not had much support from the nobles.

> ✓ Try using index cards to help you remember how Henry VII secured his throne. The first card could have questions or a numbered list for the four points: uniting, controlling, retaining and council. Then have four further cards covering the detail of each of the points.

Sample question

Try this sample essay question for yourself. A suggested answer is given at the back of the book.

Q.   (a) Describe the ways in which Henry VII controlled his nobility.   (20)

        (b) Explain how these actions helped Henry hold on to the throne.   (10)

11.2 The two pretenders

Henry's treatment of the nobles meant that he was unpopular with many of them. Because of this, the King faced several serious uprisings that threatened to remove him from the throne.

Lambert Simnel

- Edward, the Earl of Warwick, was a strong claimant to the throne, so Henry locked him up in the Tower of London.

- In 1486, Richard Symonds, an Oxford priest, began to claim that one of his pupils, named Lambert Simnel, was actually the Earl of Warwick.

- Simnel was taken to Ireland and crowned King Edward VI by his supporters. They gathered an army of Yorkists and sailed to England.

- At the Battle of East Stoke on 16th June 1487 the rebels were heavily defeated. Simnel himself was pardoned and given a job in the royal kitchens.

Perkin Warbeck

- Perkin Warbeck claimed to be Richard of York, the younger of the two 'Princes in the Tower'. He went to Ireland in 1491 and was acclaimed as the true King of England.

- In 1492–1493, he travelled around Europe gaining support and was proclaimed King Richard IV. In 1495, he went to Scotland, gained the backing of King James IV and married one of his relatives.

- Henry VII's spies reported that his old friend William Stanley was one of Warbeck's supporters and he was put to death.

- In 1497, Warbeck joined the rebellion in Cornwall (see page 62) but he was arrested and taken to London.

- When Warbeck tried to escape, he was placed in the Tower of London with the Earl of Warwick. When the two were suspected of plotting another escape, they were both put to death in November 1499.

✓ You could use a flow chart to help you remember what happened to the two pretenders. The diagram below shows what part of the chart might look like.

the two pretenders

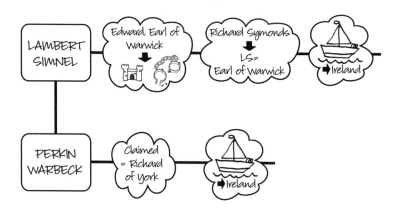

11.3 The tax rebellions

- Traditionally, people in the southern counties of England paid taxes to fund wars against France, and those in the northern counties paid to fund wars against Scotland.

- In 1489, Henry tried to gain funding for a war against France in the north as well as the south. The people of Yorkshire rebelled and killed the Earl of Northumberland.

- Henry's army managed to put down the uprising fairly easily and the rebel leaders were hanged at York.

- In 1497, the Cornish decided to rebel against taxation and gained the support of a noble, Lord Audley. They were also joined by the pretender Perkin Warbeck (see page 61).

- The Cornish rebels gathered a force and marched to London. But they were easily defeated by the King's army and the leaders were executed.

✓ Set out the main points about the tax rebellions on a chart. Use a different branch for each of the bullet points above. Remember to use pictures and different colours.

11.4 Foreign policy

- Henry's dealings with other countries reflected his desire for a secure throne. He knew that the pretenders Simnel and Warbeck had been encouraged by foreign powers.

- In 1489, Henry signed the Treaty of Medina del Campo with Spain. It was agreed that his son Arthur would marry Catherine of Aragon, the daughter of King Ferdinand of Spain. The marriage took place in 1501, but Prince Arthur died the following year.

- In 1492, Henry signed the Treaty of Etaples with France. Charles VIII of France had pledged his support for Perkin Warbeck. The English invaded France and demanded that the pretender be handed over.

- In 1502, Henry signed the Treaty of Perpetual Peace with Scotland. Henry and James IV of Scotland agreed to stop fighting each other and it was decided that James would marry Henry's daughter Margaret.

Summary

You should now know the following:

1. The methods Henry VII used to secure his place on the throne.

2. The events and consequences of the rebellions of Lambert Simnel and Perkin Warbeck.

3. The events of the tax rebellions faced by Henry VII.

4. The key points behind Henry VII's foreign policy.

Test yourself

Before moving on to the next chapter, make sure you can answer the following questions. The answers are at the back of the book.

1. What was the practice of holding a personal army called?

2. Who did Perkin Warbeck claim to be?

3. Which noble joined the Cornish tax rebels in 1497?

4. By which treaty was the marriage between Prince Arthur and Catherine of Aragon arranged?

Chapter 12: Henry VIII (1509–1547)

12.1 Early life and reign

Henry VII's elder son Arthur had died in 1502, so when the King himself died in 1509, the throne passed to his younger son, who became Henry VIII.

- Henry was not expected to become King and his father intended him to have a career in the Church. The young prince therefore became devoted to religion.

- Henry could speak Latin, French, Italian and Spanish. He loved music, composing many pieces himself, and also wrote poetry. He was also enthusiastic about works of art and architecture.

- Henry was athletic and extremely good at sports. He was strong and much taller than most men of the time.

- This age is often known as the Renaissance, which means 're-birth'. People rediscovered the beauty of classical culture from Ancient Rome and Greece, and this influenced education and the arts in particular. Henry is sometimes called a Renaissance prince.

> ✓ Draw a sketch to help you remember what happened in the early part of Henry VIII's reign and the sort of man he was. Include all the different elements of his character – the things he loved doing and what he was good at, etc.

12.2 Thomas Wolsey

Thomas Wolsey was a royal official who rose to become Henry VIII's chief minister in the early part of his reign. He became Lord Chancellor and then Archbishop of York, and was sometimes given the title *alter rex*, meaning the 'other king'.

Wolsey and finance

Henry VIII's lavish court cost money that Wolsey had to raise.

- Wolsey introduced a tax called the subsidy, which determined how much tax an individual had to pay by assessing their wealth.

- Wolsey carried on squeezing the rich nobles in the same way that Henry VII had done. They were forced to give gifts of money, known as benevolences, to the King. In return their estates and positions were secured.

- Wolsey went too far when he tried to raise money for expensive wars. In 1525, the King needed funds for a planned invasion of France, and Wolsey tried raising a tax called the Amicable Grant. There was so much opposition that it had to be abandoned.

Wolsey and law

- Wolsey re-established the Court of Star Chamber and the Court of Chancery. The Court of Requests was also re-introduced to hear cases free of charge for the poor.

- Wolsey carried out enquiries into the process of enclosure (see page 87). Because of enclosure, the lower classes were left without jobs or land. Wolsey, while supporting the process, was concerned that many landholders were doing it illegally. There were enquiries held about the issue in 1517, 1518 and 1526.

Wolsey and the Church

- In 1518, Wolsey was appointed to be the Pope's legate in England. He became determined to correct any abuses in the English Church.

- Nonetheless, he was guilty of several abuses himself. Wolsey held more than one position, which was called pluralism. Wolsey also sold church positions for money – the abuse of simony – and did not visit the areas under his control as regularly as he should have.

- In these ways, Wolsey enjoyed a lavish lifestyle. He displayed his wealth by building Hampton Court Palace.

Wolsey and foreign policy

- Wolsey's aim was to make England as important and powerful as the three main powers in Europe at that time: France, Spain and the Holy Roman Empire.

- In 1518, the leaders of all three met with Wolsey and Henry VIII in London. A peace treaty was signed and it was agreed that Henry's daughter Mary would marry Louis, the son of Francis I of France.

- Maximilian I, the Holy Roman Emperor, died in 1519 and Charles I of Spain was elected to rule his Empire as well as Spain. Henry and Francis had both hoped to become Holy Roman Emperor and now they felt threatened by Charles.

- The two kings met near Calais in June 1520. The meeting was organised by Wolsey and was an opportunity for Henry to show off his wealth and power. It became known as the 'Field of the Cloth of Gold' and was supposed to be a display of friendship, but the two kings remained wary of each other.

> ✓ Why not map out the key points in a chart to show the influence Thomas Wolsey had. Write the word 'Thomas' in the centre of the page and then draw four branches, marked finance, law, Church and foreign policy. Use pictures to sum up the key points and different colours for the different branches.

12.3 The rise of Protestantism

- The Church played an important role in everybody's life during the 16th century. But some people started to question the way it was run.

- A common practice was the selling of indulgences and the charging of money to visitors who wanted to pray over the relics of certain saints.

- The Church had gained great wealth through these practices. People began to resent the fact that this money was spent on supporting the lifestyles of churchmen, rather than being given to the poor and needy.

- Church services were conducted in Latin, which generally only priests could read. Some people started to argue that the Bible should be translated into English for ordinary people to read themselves.

- In 1517, a German monk named Martin Luther nailed a list of 95 points for reform to the door of a church in Wittenberg.

- Luther's ideas became a movement known as Protestantism. Protestants criticised practices such as the selling of indulgences and the worship of relics, and argued for translations of the Bible.

- A key argument was over the issue of bread and wine in church services. Catholics believed that the bread and wine were actually transformed into the body and blood of Christ (a process known as transubstantiation). Protestants argued that the bread and wine were only supposed to represent and commemorate the body and blood.

- Henry VIII began as a strong supporter of Catholic views. He wrote a book attacking Luther and was rewarded by the Pope with the title *Fidei Defensor*, which means 'Defender of the Faith'.

> ✓ You could plot out the rise of Protestantism in the form of a chart, with different branches for each of the different elements – problems with the Church, Martin Luther, bread and wine, Henry's views.

12.4 The King's Great Matter

In 1509, Henry VIII married Catherine of Aragon, the widow of his brother, Arthur.

- Henry wanted a strong male heir to continue the Tudor line, but the only surviving child from his marriage to Catherine of Aragon was a girl, Mary, born in 1516.

- Henry believed that he was being punished by God for marrying his brother's widow. He convinced himself that his marriage was invalid and Wolsey was instructed to seek an annulment from the Pope.

- In 1529, the Pope sent Cardinal Campeggio to England to preside over a court to debate the issue. The court failed to reach a decision.

- Henry blamed Wolsey for his failure to secure the annulment. He was charged with treason, but died in 1530 before he could be brought to trial.

- Henry appointed Thomas Cranmer to be Archbishop of Canterbury. Cranmer held many Protestant views and was known to support an annulment. He secretly married Henry and Anne Boleyn in January 1533 and annulled the marriage to Catherine.

- The Pope excommunicated Henry. But Henry now believed that he, and not the Pope, should be in charge of the Church in England.

- In September 1533, Anne gave birth to Henry's child. To the King's huge disappointment, it was another girl – Elizabeth.

Evidence question

You may be asked to answer an evidence question on Henry VIII and his Great Matter. Refer to the guidance on pages xi–xii and make sure that you practise answering these questions.

12.5 Cromwell and the Reformation

Thomas Cromwell was Henry's chief advisor and, like Cranmer, was sympathetic to the Protestant cause. In what has since become known as the Reformation Parliament, Cromwell used his influence to pass several laws.

The Reformation Parliament

- The Act in Restraint of Annates (1532) stopped the English Church making payments to the Pope.

- The Statute in Restraint of Appeals (1533) declared that England was ruled by a king who had 'whole and entire authority' within it. Therefore any excommunications from Rome of English people were invalid and the English were forbidden from appealing to the Pope.

- The Act of Succession (1533) declared that the marriage of Henry VIII and Catherine of Aragon had been invalid and that Princess Mary was therefore illegitimate. The Act stated that the throne would pass to the children of Henry and Anne Boleyn instead.

- The Act of Supremacy (1534) declared that Henry was the head of the English Church, not the Pope.

- The Treason Act (1534) stated that anyone who argued against Henry's position as head of the English Church would face a charge of treason. Two victims of this law were John Fisher, the Bishop of Rochester, and Sir Thomas More, Henry's former Lord Chancellor. Both men were executed in 1535.

- The First Fruits and Tenths Act (1534) allowed Henry to take the first year's earnings from all bishoprics and church offices. Thereafter he would take one-tenth of any further earnings.

✓ Think up a silly story, using the first letters of each of the Acts, to help you remember the order they were passed:

Act of **R**estraint of **An**nates (1532)   RANdy

Statute in **R**estraint of **Ap**peals (1533)   RAPper

Act of **Suc**cession (1533)   SUCked down his

Act of **Sup**remacy (1534)   SoUP with

Treason Act (1534)   TREAcle,

First **Frui**ts and **Te**nths Act (1534)   FRUIT and TEa

See *Study Skills*, page 66 for help with this.

Dissolution of the Monasteries

The 'break with Rome' provoked the Catholic countries of Spain and France to declare war on England, which was encouraged by the Pope. Henry now needed money to defend England.

● In the 1520s, Cromwell had helped Thomas Wolsey to close down the most corrupt monasteries. He now believed that the process could be continued and all the wealth of these houses given over to the Crown.

● In 1536, Parliament passed the First Act of Dissolution that allowed the smaller monasteries to be closed down. This was followed in 1539 by the Second Act of Dissolution, which dealt with the larger monasteries.

● Local landowners were very pleased to buy the land and buildings of the monastery for their own uses.

The Pilgrimage of Grace

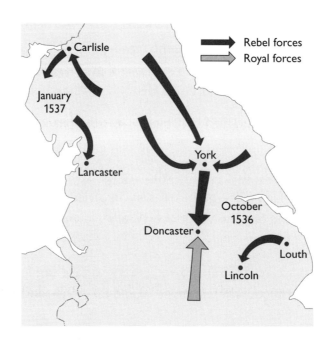

68

The opposition to the Dissolution of the Monasteries came from local people who took up arms against Cromwell's men.

- At Lincoln in 1536, a force of 10,000 men attacked the commissioners and occupied the cathedral.

- In Yorkshire, a lawyer named Robert Aske and a noble named Lord Darcy gathered 30,000 men together. The movement became known as the Pilgrimage of Grace.

- Aske drew up a petition in December 1536, calling for an end to heresy and declaring that Princess Mary was legitimate.

- Aske marched south with his men, claiming to be leading a pilgrimage, not a rebellion. He declared that they did not intend to attack the King but to free him from the influences of advisors like Cromwell.

- The Duke of Norfolk met the rebels at Doncaster and promised to hold a Parliament to discuss their complaints. But Henry had no intention of keeping these promises and the ringleaders were executed.

Sample question

Try this sample essay question for yourself. A suggested answer is given at the back of the book.

Q.   (a) Describe the events of the Pilgrimage of Grace.   (20)

         (b) Explain why the rebels were not able to succeed.   (10)

The Ten Articles (1536) and the Six Articles (1539)

Cromwell wanted to make the English Church more Protestant and urged Parliament to pass the Act of Ten Articles in 1536.

- The Church now only recognised three sacraments: baptism, penance and the eucharist. The Bible was translated into English and priests were allowed to marry.

- The other Catholic sacraments of confirmation, ordination, marriage and the last rites were now no longer regarded as holy sacraments. Pilgrimages and the display of relics were also banned.

But despite his treatment of the Church, Henry still regarded himself as Catholic. Cromwell was in danger of making England a wholly Protestant country, which the King did not want. So in 1539, the Ten Articles were modified by the Six Articles, which reintroduced many Catholic beliefs.

- The idea of transubstantiation was confirmed. The people could now take only bread at the Communion, not wine, and were encouraged to confess their sins to a priest. Priests were once again banned from marrying.

- Henry produced the King's Book, which prohibited many kinds of people from reading the new English Bible.

12.6 The six wives of Henry VIII

The fates of Henry VIII's six wives can be remembered by means of a well-known ditty:

Divorced, beheaded, died;
divorced, beheaded, survived.

Catherine of Aragon

- Catherine was Henry's first wife. Henry had their marriage annulled when it became obvious she was not going to produce a son.

Anne Boleyn

- Anne had given Henry a daughter, Elizabeth, but she was the only one of their children who survived. Henry became convinced that he was being punished. He had also fallen in love with another courtier, Jane Seymour, and wanted to be rid of his wife.

- Cromwell accused Anne of treason, adultery and incest – charges that are now believed to be untrue. She was tried, found guilty and executed in May 1536.

Jane Seymour

- Henry then married Jane Seymour and in October 1536 she gave birth to a boy, whom the delighted King named Edward.

- However, soon after the birth, Jane developed puerperal fever and died 12 days later.

Anne of Cleves

- It was suggested that Henry marry Anne of Cleves for political reasons. Henry decided to marry her based on her portrait by Hans Holbein.

- A few days before the wedding, Henry met Anne and was not impressed. By this time, it was impossible to back out and the ceremony went ahead. Henry and Anne agreed to annul the marriage six months later.

Catherine Howard

- Henry was angry with Cromwell for the part he had played in the marriage to Anne of Cleves. He was accused of heresy and executed in July 1540.

- Henry married Catherine Howard in the same month. However, Catherine committed adultery against the King. She was tried for treason, found guilty and executed in February 1542.

Catherine Parr

- Henry married Catherine Parr in July 1543. She persuaded him to make amends with his two daughters.

- Henry's will, made on 30th December 1546, declared that the throne would pass first to his son Edward, then to any children he might have with Catherine Parr, then to Mary, Elizabeth and the daughters of his sister Mary Rose.

Henry VIII died a month later, on 28th January 1547 and his throne passed to his nine-year-old son, who became Edward VI.

> ✓ Try using a chart with separate sections to help you remember the details about Henry VIII's wives. Have a different branch/section for each of the wives.

Summary

You should now know the following:

1. The events of Henry VIII's early life and the main points of his personality.

2. The influence of Thomas Wolsey on Henry VIII's government.

3. The key ideas of Protestantism and the events surrounding its rise.

4. The events and consequences of the annulment of Henry VIII's marriage to Catherine of Aragon.

5. The acts of Thomas Cromwell and the events of the English Reformation.

6. The events surrounding the marriages and fates of Henry VIII's six wives.

Test yourself

Before moving on to the next chapter, make sure you can answer the following questions. The answers are at the back of the book.

1. What were benevolences?

2. What was the name of the meeting between Henry VIII and Francis I near Calais in June 1520?

3. Why was Henry VIII awarded the title *Fidei Defensor*?

4. Why did Henry VIII want his marriage to Catherine of Aragon to be annulled?

5. Which Act of Parliament allowed Henry VIII to take a portion of the earnings from church offices?

6. The Act of Ten Articles allowed which three church sacraments to be recognised?

Chapter 13: Edward VI (1547–1553) and Mary I (1553–1558)

13.1 Edward VI and the Protestant surge

Edward's tutors were sympathetic to Protestant ideas and Edward was very much influenced by them. He was too young to rule when Henry VIII died, so the country was run by his uncle Edward Seymour, the Duke of Somerset, and John Dudley, the Duke of Northumberland. Both were also keen Protestants.

Thomas Cranmer

- Cranmer now set out to get rid of Catholicism entirely. Certain ceremonies, processions and rituals were banned.

- The Chantries Act (1547) abolished chantries and their wealth was diverted to the Crown.

- The Act of Uniformity (1549) made English the official language of the Church and stated that both bread and wine should be distributed to the people at Communion.

- Cranmer drew up the *Book of Common Prayer* in 1549. He attempted to tone down the Catholic idea of transubstantiation by neither rejecting nor entirely supporting it.

- Meanwhile, Protestant ideas in Europe were being strengthened by the teachings of John Calvin. Calvin argued that church services should be as plain and simple as possible, with the role of the priest (or minister) much reduced.

- Calvin's views influenced the ideas of extreme Protestants who became known as Puritans. They believed in devoting one's life completely to God, avoiding all kinds of entertainment, and removing ornaments and decoration from churches.

- Cranmer recognised that strong Protestants were unsatisfied with his 1549 Prayer Book. He therefore revised it in 1552, with an edition that was more Calvinist: for example, the idea of transubstantiation was dismissed.

- The following year, Cranmer published the Forty-Two Articles, which were entirely Protestant.

> ✓ You could try making up a story that connects the important points about Thomas Cranmer's influence and how things changed in the Church during this time. Make the story as vivid as possible so that all the main points come to life in your head.

The 1549 rebellions

- The Western Rebellion, in April 1549, started in Devon and Cornwall. The rebels were protesting about the introduction of the Book of Common Prayer. They also disagreed with the abolition of chantries and the raising of new taxes.

- The rebels demanded the reinstatement of the Six Articles of 1539 and a return to Catholic worship.

- The city of Exeter was surrounded and placed under siege for over a month. A government force relieved the city and 2,500 people were killed in several small battles that followed.

- Kett's Rebellion, in July 1549, began in East Anglia. The rebels were protesting about the process of enclosure and the cost of renting land.

- Led by Robert Kett, a force of rebels occupied the city of Norwich. Eventually a large force, led by John Dudley, the Earl of Warwick (later the Duke of Northumberland), defeated the rebels in battle at Mousehold Heath. About 3,000 of Kett's men were killed and Kett was executed in December 1549.

13.2 Lady Jane Grey and Mary I

Edward became ill in his early teens and by 1553, aged fifteen, he was not expected to survive long. He was therefore encouraged to name his successor.

- According to the terms of Henry VIII's will, his eldest daughter Mary was to follow Edward. But the Duke of Northumberland urged the King not to agree to this. Mary was known to be a devout Catholic and Northumberland was a staunch Protestant.

- Cranmer also knew that Mary, if she came to the throne, would reverse all the work he had done to dismantle Catholicism in England.

- Northumberland persuaded Edward to name Lady Jane Grey as the heir to the throne in his will. Jane was married to Guildford Dudley, Northumberland's son.

- Edward died of tuberculosis in July 1553 and Northumberland claimed the throne on Jane's behalf on 10th July. Nine days later, Mary rode into London. She had the support of the people and Parliament declared her the rightful Queen.

- Jane and her husband were imprisoned in the Tower of London and Northumberland was arrested and executed the following month. Thomas Cranmer was arrested in September and also thrown in the Tower.

Mary I had had a difficult childhood, having to endure the public divorce of her parents and being disowned by her father as illegitimate. She had maintained her strict Catholic faith despite the movement towards Protestantism.

- Mary was determined to return Catholicism to England. She believed that the public support for her accession to the throne showed that the people wanted this as well.

- Mary needed to produce a Catholic heir and decided to marry her cousin Philip, who was soon to become King Philip II of Spain. The Prince was invited to England in 1554.

✓ You could use a flow chart to remember the events leading to Mary I becoming Queen. Use different rows to show what happened to Edward, Northumberland, Lady Jane Grey and Mary. You could start it like the one below. Think what you would put in the first bubbles for Lady Jane Grey and Mary, and add extra bubbles for all the other key points you need to remember.

Mary I's accession

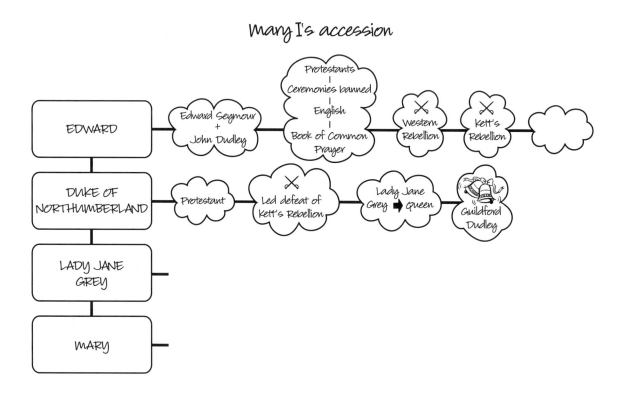

13.3 Wyatt's Rebellion (1554)

- Sir Thomas Wyatt hatched a plot to remove Mary from the throne and replace her with her second cousin Edward Courtenay. Edward would then take Mary's half-sister Elizabeth as his queen.

- Wyatt gathered 3,000 men and they marched into London. However, Mary was able to persuade the people of London to stay loyal to her.

- The rebellion failed and the ringleaders were executed. Elizabeth swore that she had not been involved but was imprisoned at Woodstock Manor in Oxfordshire.

- Mary became worried that Lady Jane Grey would become a focus for any future attempts to overthrow her. Jane and her husband, Guildford Dudley, were therefore both executed for treason in February 1554.

- Mary was married to Philip in July 1554 and he became King of Spain 18 months later, making Mary Queen of both England and Spain.

13.4 The Catholic resurgence

With Wyatt's Rebellion crushed, Mary set out to restore Catholicism to England.

- Reginald Pole, a devout Catholic, was appointed Archbishop of Canterbury. Together Mary and Pole persuaded Parliament to revoke the religious laws passed since 1529.

- The Pope became head of the Church once more, priests were banned from marrying, services were held in Latin and decoration returned to churches.

- Mary also restored the old law that heretics who spoke out against the Church were to be burned at the stake. From February 1555 onwards, priests, bishops, men, women and children were publicly burned.

- It is believed that nearly 300 people died in this way during Mary's reign. Their deaths were later recorded in *Acts and Monuments* by John Foxe, better known as the *Book of Martyrs*.

- The most notable death was that of Thomas Cranmer in 1556. He had initially signed documents swearing to uphold Catholic teachings. But he went back on his word, declaring that he still held his Protestant views, and was burned in March 1556.

Evidence question

You may be asked to answer an evidence question on Mary I and the Protestants. Refer to the guidance on pages xi–xii and make sure that you practise answering these questions.

Mary died in November 1558 and, as her marriage to Philip had not produced a son, the throne passed to her half-sister Elizabeth.

Summary

You should now know the following:

1. The events of the Protestant surge during the reign of Edward VI.

2. The events surrounding the succession of Lady Jane Grey and Mary I.

3. The events and consequences of Wyatt's Rebellion.

4. The events of the Catholic resurgence during the reign of Mary I.

Test yourself

Before moving on to the next chapter, make sure you can answer the following questions. The answers are at the back of the book.

1. Which French theologian argued for a more radical form of Protestantism than Martin Luther?

2. For how many days did Lady Jane Grey reign unofficially as Queen?

3. What was the main reason for the failure of Wyatt's rebellion?

4. Which famous book recorded the execution of Protestants during the reign of Mary I?

Chapter 14: Elizabeth I (1558–1603)

14.1 Early life and reign

Like her half-sister Mary, Elizabeth had a difficult childhood. Her mother, Anne Boleyn, was executed and Elizabeth had been declared illegitimate.

- Like her father, Elizabeth was intelligent, artistic and musical. As a moderate Protestant, she was suspected of being the focus of anti-Catholic plots during the reign of Mary I and was imprisoned.

- According to the terms of her father's will, Elizabeth gained the throne on the death of Mary in November 1588.

Elizabeth had to deal with four main problems during her reign.

The threat of invasion

- King Francis II of France claimed that Elizabeth was illegitimate. He was married to the Catholic Mary I of Scotland, usually known today as Mary, Queen of Scots. He claimed that his wife, as the nearest legitimate descendant of Henry VII, was the true Queen of England.

- Francis died in 1560, but the Kings of France and Spain continued to threaten an invasion.

The religious divide

- The reigns of Henry VIII, Edward VI and Mary I had seen a religious 'merry-go-round'. Catholics and Protestants were equally confused about all the changes and simply wanted to worship as they wished.

- Though a Protestant herself, Elizabeth had to find a way to keep both sides as happy as possible.

The issue of succession

- Generally, Catholics had not supported the marriage of Henry VIII and Anne Boleyn. They therefore believed that Elizabeth was illegitimate. Many others believed that a woman was unsuited to ruling the country.

- The easiest way to solve these problems was for Elizabeth to marry and give birth to a legitimate heir.

The lack of money

- When Elizabeth came to the throne, her treasury was severely lacking in funds. England needed money to defend against the threat of foreign invasion.

- There had also been poor harvests and the number of beggars had increased.

14.2 The Elizabethan Settlement

Elizabeth tried to solve the religious divide in a way that would include as many people as possible. In 1559 she enacted two pieces of law.

The Act of Supremacy (1559)

● The Act of Supremacy established Elizabeth as the Supreme Governor of the Church of England.

● The wording of the Act was important. Elizabeth claimed to be the Supreme *Governor*, not the Supreme *Head* of the Church. This allowed Catholics to believe that the Pope was still in charge of the Church worldwide.

The Act of Uniformity (1559)

● The Act of Uniformity introduced a new version of the *Book of Common Prayer*, which was based on Cranmer's 1552 version, but with some subtle differences.

● Priests were made to wear vestments, but these were toned down. People had to attend church on Sundays and holy days, or risk being fined.

● The difficult issue of transubstantiation was open to interpretation. The wording now allowed people to believe either that the bread and wine had become the body and blood of Christ, or that this happened only for true believers, or that Christ was simply being commemorated.

Elizabeth replaced the more extremist bishops with men of more moderate views, such as the Archbishop of Canterbury Matthew Parker.

The Thirty-Nine Articles

● The Thirty-Nine Articles, agreed in 1563 and passed by Parliament in 1571, were based on Cranmer's Forty-Two Articles of 1553.

● They abolished certain Catholic beliefs, such as the idea of transubstantiation, and supported Protestant ideas such as clerical marriage. They established Elizabeth's Church of England as moderately Protestant.

Puritans and Catholics

Elizabeth had designed her settlement to appeal to as many moderate people as possible. But there were still extremists on either side who would not accept any compromise.

- There were several Puritan members of Parliament and in 1571 they pushed to make the *Book of Common Prayer* more radical. When this did not work, the Puritans published their own alternative Prayer Book in 1574.

- Elizabeth was just as wary about the extreme Catholics – mostly because they had powerful support in the Kings of France and Spain.

- There were a number of Catholic plots against Elizabeth (see page 80), many of which were focused on placing Mary, Queen of Scots on the English throne. Elizabeth appointed Sir Francis Walsingham to be the head of her security service.

- Jesuits were sheltered by rich Catholic families who built priestholes in their homes for them to hide in.

> ✓ Why not use index cards to help you remember the main points of the Elizabethan Settlement or you could try another mnemonic. For example:
>
> Super Uni had 39 Articles

Sample question

Try this sample essay question for yourself. A suggested answer is given at the back of the book.

Q. (a) Describe the main points of the Elizabethan Settlement. (20)

   (b) Explain how Elizabeth hoped to appeal to both moderate Catholics
       and Protestants. (10)

14.3 Mary, Queen of Scots

Mary, Queen of Scots, was the daughter of James V of Scotland, who was himself the son of Henry VII's daughter Margaret Tudor (see the family tree on page 200).

- Mary became Queen of Scotland at less than a year old. She married Francis, the son of the King of France, in 1559. He became King the following year but died shortly afterwards.

- Mary's second marriage was to her cousin Henry, Lord Darnley. Darnley believed that Mary was having an affair with her secretary, an Italian named David Rizzio.

- Darnley arranged Rizzio's murder in March 1566 and was himself murdered in February 1567. Suspicion fell on Mary and her lover, the Earl of Bothwell.

- The Scottish nobles turned against them and imprisoned Mary in Lochleven Castle, where she was forced to abdicate the throne in favour of her infant son, James.

- Mary managed to escape to England and to the court of Elizabeth, who decided to keep Mary imprisoned, although in relative comfort.

But while Mary was still alive, Catholic plotters saw her as a possible replacement for Elizabeth on the throne.

The Northern Rebellion (1569)

- A leading Catholic family, the Howards of Norfolk, wanted Elizabeth to name Mary as her successor. When Elizabeth found out, the Duke of Norfolk was imprisoned in the Tower of London.

- The Earls of Northumberland and Westmorland, who had supported the marriage plans, took control of much of Yorkshire and the north-east of England.

- The rebellion was put down by a force led by the Earl of Sussex. Westmorland fled abroad, and Northumberland was captured and executed in 1572.

The Ridolfi Plot (1571)

- In 1571, a wealthy Italian banker named Roberto di Ridolfi hatched a plot to break Mary out of prison, marry her to the Duke of Norfolk and place her on the throne.

- Sir Francis Walsingham uncovered the plot and managed to arrest Norfolk, who was thrown into the Tower again.

- Ridolfi was never captured. Mary denied all involvement, but the Duke of Norfolk was executed in June 1572.

The Throckmorton Plot (1583)

- In 1583, a Catholic named Francis Throckmorton was caught taking letters, supposedly written by Mary, to the Spanish ambassador asking for help from Spain.

- Throckmorton was executed, but it could not be proved that Mary had actually written the letters herself, and she was once again spared.

The Babington Plot (1586)

- In 1586, letters to Mary from a Catholic named Anthony Babington were intercepted by Walsingham's spies. They showed that Babington was plotting to kill Elizabeth and replace her with Mary.

- Mary was put on trial for treason at Fotheringhay Castle and was found guilty.

Elizabeth was still reluctant to execute her cousin. She later claimed that Mary's death warrant had been sent against her wishes. Mary, Queen of Scots, was executed on 8th February 1587.

> ✓ Try charting what happened to Mary, Queen of Scots, from becoming Queen at less than a year old to her final execution. Include branches for the different plots and rebellions.

14.4 War with Spain

- Philip II of Spain was keen to keep England a Catholic country and felt that the easiest way to do this was to marry Elizabeth. But his offer of marriage was refused.

- In 1579, Elizabeth considered marrying the Duke of Alençon, who was Philip's enemy. When Philip conquered Portugal in 1580, Elizabeth supported his rival for the Portugese throne.

- The Spanish were also said to be involved in several of the Catholic plots against Elizabeth (see page 80).

- English ships threatened the Spanish trade in South America. In 1569, the adventurer Sir Francis Drake raided Spanish trading ships and seized their treasures.

The Spanish Armada (1588)

Philip had been planning an invasion of England since 1586. Thanks to a network of spies, the English knew this and were able to take measures to defend the country.

- In 1587, Sir Francis Drake led a raiding party to the Spanish port of Cadiz. Thirty Spanish ships were destroyed, in an action that became known as 'singeing the King of Spain's beard'. This delayed the Spanish invasion for a year.

- The Spanish fleet was ready to sail in 1588. Philip had gathered an army of 30,000 men in the Netherlands and he wanted to destroy the English ships in the Channel, allowing his army to cross to England safely.

- Philip appointed the Duke of Medina Sidonia as the commander of the Armada. He was brave and a good organiser, but lacked experience.

The Spanish left the port of Corunna on 22nd July 1588 and were sighted off Plymouth on 30th July.

- The Spanish tactic was to make a crescent-shaped formation, with heavy cargo ships in the middle and large warships at either side. The English ships were smaller, but faster and more manoeuvrable, with cannon that could fire a greater distance.

- The two sides fought several small battles, but neither side suffered much damage, and the Spanish continued towards the narrowest part of the Channel to meet their soldiers.

- When the Spanish fleet reached this point, they found that the army was not ready to cross. The Spanish were forced to anchor off Calais and hope that their soldiers were ready before the English ships reached them.

- On 7th August, the English set fire to eight ships and allowed them to drift into the anchored Spanish fleet. The Spanish cut their anchors and sailed north, away from Calais.

- The English now met the disorganised Spanish fleet in battle, off the town of Gravelines in France. It was the bloodiest battle of the whole campaign, with many Spanish ships badly damaged.

- The Duke of Medina Sidonia gave the order to continue north. The English followed for several days, then turned back.

- The Spanish continued around the British Isles but their sailors were weakened with disease and hunger. Many ships were wrecked in storms. In all, the Spanish lost 60 ships and 11,000 men.

- To Elizabeth, the Armada was a huge political success and reinforced her standing as a strong monarch.

14.5 Elizabeth's government

If she was to solve the four problems she encountered at the start of her reign, Elizabeth had to make sure that she enjoyed good relations with her government.

William Cecil, Lord Burghley

- William Cecil was Elizabeth's closest advisor. As Lord Treasurer, he helped to reduce the spending of the government and opened up new trade routes between England and other countries (see page 85).

- Cecil became the Queen's spokesman in Parliament and managed both to represent her wishes to the MPs and keep her informed of the mood of Parliament.

- Cecil also advised on foreign policy, trying to avoid war and reach agreement by diplomatic means. At the same time, he made sure that enough money was spent on keeping England's defences secure.

- He was determined not to let a Catholic back on to the English throne and is considered to have been the main influence in having Mary, Queen of Scots executed.

Elizabeth and Parliament

- Elizabeth called Parliament ten times during her reign, always either to pass laws or raise taxes. She understood that they had the right to debate matters of state, but always resented any interference in finance, religion or the issue of succession.

- When MPs pressed her to marry and produce an heir, Elizabeth became more determined to resist them. Those who interfered in religious matters were even arrested and placed in the Tower of London.

- Elizabeth knew that she needed Parliament to pass important Acts. Generally, she was able to maintain good relations with Parliament and, in return, she was respected for it.

Ireland and rebellion

The wars in Ireland

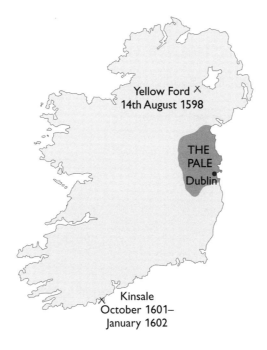

- Elizabeth's good relations with her government were vital in dealing with trouble in Ireland. Her officials controlled an area of land around Dublin known as the Pale. The rest of Ireland was controlled by independent nobles.

- Ireland had also remained Catholic and was therefore a potential base from which a foreign Catholic country could launch an invasion of England.

- In 1598, an Irish noble named Hugh O'Neill, the Earl of Tyrone, defeated an English force at the Battle of Yellow Ford. This allowed him to rule over much of Ireland.

- Elizabeth's favourite, the Earl of Essex, was sent to restore English authority to Ireland. But this campaign was a dismal failure and Essex returned to England. He blamed Elizabeth's ministers for turning the Queen against him and, in 1601, gathered a small rebel force to fight in London. This failed, too, and he was executed for treason.

- In the meantime, Lord Mountjoy had more success in Ireland. He defeated the Irish in a series of battles at Kinsale during the winter of 1601–1602.

Elizabeth died in 1603, having dealt effectively with most of the problems that she had encountered. Her army and navy had successfully fought off any attempts to invade. The Elizabethan Settlement had proved to be an inclusive way of bringing about religious harmony, at least for the time being. And, while foreign wars had been expensive, the economy was much more stable than at the beginning of her reign. But one problem remained: the question of who would succeed her. Elizabeth never married and had no children. On her deathbed, she named as her choice the son of Mary, Queen of Scots, King James VI of Scotland. He came to the English throne as James I of England.

Summary

You should now know the following:

1.   The four main problems facing Elizabeth I during her reign.

2.   The terms of the Elizabethan Settlement.

3.   The events surrounding the imprisonment and execution of Mary, Queen of Scots.

4.   The events of Elizabeth I's war with Spain.

5.   The acts of Elizabeth's government.

Test yourself

Before moving on to the next chapter, make sure you can answer the following questions. The answers are at the back of the book.

1.   How did the Act of Supremacy (1559) make a small concession to Catholics?

2.   Who was the head of Elizabeth I's secret service?

3.   Which battle was the bloodiest of the Spanish Armada campaign of 1588?

4.   Which noble led the Irish uprising against Elizabeth I during the years 1598–1602?

Chapter 15: Life in the 16th century

15.1 Trade

In the 16th century, England began to change from a country in which the wealth came from the land (agriculture), to one in which the wealth came from the sale of manufactured goods (trade).

- By the Elizabethan period, England was trading successfully with other countries in Europe. English cloth was popular in France and the Netherlands. Other materials, such as iron, salt, sugar, coal and wool, were sent all over Europe.

- English ports became more important. Towns such as Bristol and Liverpool became industrialised, and grew quickly.

- Merchants gained their wealth by buying the materials from locals in England, manufacturing the goods and selling them to foreign buyers at a higher price.

- As adventurers including Sir Francis Drake explored far-away countries such as the Americas, new trade routes opened up and produced more opportunities for merchants.

- These expeditions were risky and merchants began to join together and form joint stock companies.

- The merchants sold shares in these companies to rich landowners and the government promised these companies a monopoly if they opened up trade routes to new countries.

- London's docks grew as more quays were built for loading and unloading. Elizabeth introduced legal quays with the sole right to receive goods from overseas.

✓ Draw a picture to depict the growth in trade during the Elizabethan period or make up a story. Include all the different elements from the growth of different towns to the explorers such as Sir Francis Drake.

15.2 Poverty and the Poor Laws

The 16th century also saw a huge increase in the number of poor people in England. One cause for this was the lack of jobs and there were several reasons for this:

- The enclosure movement (see page 87) and the change from arable to pastoral farming meant that a much smaller workforce was needed.

- The Dissolution of the Monasteries meant that people who had previously been monks and nuns now had to find work.

- The clampdown on retaining meant that soldiers were left without work.

- The population of England rose by over 1 million in the 16th century.

The rate of inflation during the 16th century

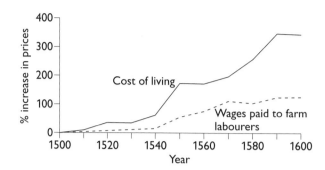

Another cause of poverty was the rise in inflation and there were several reasons for this.

- There was increased demand for everyday foods, but not enough to go around. The price of this food rose as people competed to buy it.

- Governments debased the coinage, reducing the amount of precious metal in each coin.

- Foreign wars were expensive to fund.

- There were a number of bad harvests.

The governments of Henry VIII, Edward VI and Mary I did not take steps to stop people being poor in the first place. They were more concerned with the threat to law and order posed by beggars.

- In 1547, Parliament passed an Act declaring that vagrants could be branded, whipped and sent back to their home parish. Some were imprisoned or even killed.

In 1597 and 1601, the government of Elizabeth I passed a series of Poor Laws. These were enacted to offer help to the poorest people. They defined two classes of poor:

- The deserving poor were those unable to work. A tax called the Poor Rate was collected from the rich by the Overseers of the Poor. This money helped the deserving poor, either through indoor relief in the parish poorhouse or by outdoor relief in their own homes.

- The idle poor – those who did not work because they were lazy – were to be whipped and sent back to their home parish. If they carried on begging they were sent to a House of Correction or even hanged.

15.3 Town and country

Towns

- The growth in trade had caused many towns to grow quickly. London, for example, had a population of 60,000 in 1500 but had grown to 250,000 just 100 years later.

- Tudor towns were filthy, with rubbish and sewage lying in the streets. Disease spread quickly through the town.

Homes

- In the 16th century, a large, beautiful home was a sign of the owner's prestige and wealth. The rich built large and ornate houses, some of which survive today.

- These houses were made mostly of timber, with the roof being thatched or tiled. They contained huge, heavy pieces of furniture, usually made of oak, which lasted for generations.

- The poor still lived in very simple houses with only one or two rooms. Furniture was very basic and most people slept on the bare earth floor.

Pastimes

- Music and dancing were very popular in Tudor times. The richer households owned keyboard instruments such as the spinet or virginals. Poorer people sometimes played the lute or flute.

- Sports were also common in towns and villages, especially team sports such as football. Thankfully, sports such as bear-baiting and cock-fighting have been outlawed today.

- The theatre was also popular and this encouraged the writing of famous plays by Marlowe, Johnson and – of course – Shakespeare (see page 108).

Enclosure

- Enclosure was a two-part process: first, the division of open fields; second, the enclosure of the common land.

- In medieval times, England used an open-field system, in which farmers rented a strip of land on a large field. Enclosure meant that the lords withdrew the lease of the land and enclosed the field for grazing animals.

- The lords also fenced off the common land and began to use it for their own livestock.

- The local people resented the changes and this sometimes provoked revolts such as Kett's Rebellion (see page 73).

- Enclosure allowed the wool trade to grow. The government raised more money through the taxes paid on exporting wool to foreign countries.

✓ You could map out what life was like in the towns and countryside of Elizabethan England. Use a different branch for each of the headings above. You should be able to include lots of different pictures instead of words to help you visualise what went on. Try using the one below as a starting point and add in the sub-branches.

Life in Elizabethan England

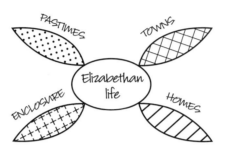

Sample question

Try this sample essay question for yourself. A suggested answer is given at the back of the book.

Q. (a) Describe the process of enclosure. (20)

(b) Explain why this process led to unrest in the countryside. (10)

15.4 Women in the 16th century

The role of women had not changed much since medieval times. Women were still believed to be inferior to men and it was this way of thinking that had made Henry VIII so determined to have a male heir.

- A husband was legally responsible for all his family. He was allowed to sell off any land and property that his wife had owned before their marriage. If she committed adultery, she could be punished severely.

- Girls were generally only taught how to perform household tasks. These tasks would include cooking and food preparation, cleaning, washing and sewing. Only very rich women were taught to read and write.

- Marriages were often carried out to increase the wealth of both families. The bride gave a dowry as a contribution to the household, which might have been a gift of money, land or property.

- Pregnancy was dangerous and the death of the mother during childbirth was not uncommon. Even if a birth was successful, the mother could contract a post-natal illness, such as puerperal fever.

- The wives of rich husbands spent much of their time at leisure, though they did have to make sure that their servants were running the household properly.

- Poorer women had to look after the children and cook meals themselves, and often had to help their husbands working in the fields.

- Women dressed both to suit the Tudor fashions and to show off their wealth. The clothes were sometimes very ornate and heavy.

Summary

You should now know the following:

1.   The reasons for the growth in trade during the 16th century.

2.   The reasons for the growth in poverty and the provisions of the Elizabethan Poor Laws.

3.   The key characteristics of towns, homes and pastimes, and the process of enclosure in the 16th century.

4.   The position of women in the 16th century.

Test yourself

Before moving on to the next chapter, make sure you can answer the following questions. The answers are at the back of the book.

1.   How could companies obtain a monopoly?

2.   What was the difference between the deserving poor and the idle poor?

3.   How did the process of enclosure provide more money for the government through taxes?

4.   What was the main household task for the wives of rich husbands?

Chapter 16: James I (1603–1625) and Charles I (1625–1649)

16.1 James I and religion

Unlike his mother, Mary, Queen of Scots, James was brought up as a Protestant. He became James VI of Scotland at the age of one, when his mother was forced to abdicate the Scottish throne and pass power to him. When Elizabeth died, James was proclaimed King James I of England.

- Puritans hoped that James would stamp out Catholicism in England once and for all. The Millenary Petition demanded the removal of bishops and alterations to make the *Book of Common Prayer* more radical.

- But at a Church conference at Hampton Court Palace in 1604, James refused to dismiss the bishops.

- Some Puritans decided to leave England to start a new life elsewhere. One group of these were the Pilgrim Fathers, who sailed to America in the *Mayflower* in September 1620.

- James did agree to a new English translation of the Bible. This work was called the *Authorised Version* and is today often known as the King James Bible.

> ✓ Use pictures to help you remember the main points with regard to James I and religion. You could draw a series of sketches depicting, for example, James refusing to dismiss the bishops and the Pilgrim Fathers setting sail for America.

The Gunpowder Plot (1605)

- In 1604, two Catholics named Robert Catesby and Thomas Percy devised a plan to assassinate James by blowing up the Houses of Parliament as he opened the session. The date for the attempt was to be 5th November 1605.

- On 26th October 1605, another plotter named Francis Tresham wrote to his brother-in-law Lord Monteagle, warning him not to attend the opening of Parliament for his own safety. Monteagle passed the letter on to the authorities.

- On the night of 4th November, a plotter named Guy Fawkes was arrested in a cellar underneath Parliament. Under torture, he revealed the names of the conspirators and within a few days they had all been arrested or killed in skirmishes. They were hanged, drawn and quartered the following year.

- Some historians suggest that the men were framed by James's government and the false plot was invented as an excuse to pass anti-Catholic laws.

✓ Most people can remember the rhyme about the Gunpowder Plot:

Remember, remember the fifth of November
Gunpowder, treason and plot.
I see no reason why gunpowder, treason
Should ever be forgot …

Try making up a phrase or rhyme to help you remember the people involved in the plot:

Robert Catesby
Thomas Percy
Francis Tresham
Guy Fawkes

16.2 James I and Parliament

James firmly believed in the Divine Right of Kings, which declared that monarchs had their right to rule given to them by God. This attitude was to colour his dealings with Parliament.

- James himself proved to be an extravagant king who lived well and spent money unwisely. Consequently, he often had to ask Parliament for more funds.

- As King of England and Scotland, James had joined the two crowns in a personal union, but he also had an ambition to merge the two countries formally as one and declare himself the first King of Great Britain.

- When in 1604 he asked Parliament to approve this move and give him more money to finance the continuing war with Spain, Parliament refused and James ended the session.

- James started selling titles, such as peerages and knighthoods, and monopolies to companies. Parliament claimed that these actions were illegal.

- James called the Addled Parliament in 1614, but ended it only eight weeks later when it resisted his wishes to raise taxes.

- George Villiers, the Duke of Buckingham, rose to power through his friendship with the King. He advised James on his policies.

- James called a third Parliament in 1621, which he dissolved when Parliament tried to debate foreign policy and the proposed marriage between his son Charles and the daughter of the King of Spain, which the members did not support because she was Catholic.

- James's final Parliament, in 1624, was called in desperation to raise money. The Lord Treasurer, Sir Lionel Cranfield, was trying to stabilise the spending but Parliament had him removed from office. Parliament also agreed to give money for a war with Spain, which James did not support.

James I died in March 1625 and the throne passed to his son Charles.

16.3 Charles I and religion

Charles I was known to favour High Anglicanism, a Church that was Protestant but retained much of the splendour and ceremony of the Catholic Church.

- Charles married Henrietta Maria, the daughter of the King of France, who was Catholic. His marriage alarmed Parliament, who believed that he would move England towards Catholicism once more.

- Charles was a believer in the Divine Right of Kings and refused to allow people to question his decisions.

- In 1633, William Laud was appointed Archbishop of Canterbury. Laud was a High Anglican and upheld the role of bishops, allowed priests to wear vestments, and reintroduced old ceremonies and decorations into churches.

- Laud also persecuted Puritan radicals who opposed him. In 1637, three Puritans named William Prynne, Henry Burton and John Bastwick were tortured (they had their ears cut off) for speaking against him. The following year, a pamphleteer named 'Freeborn John' Lilburne was arrested.

The First Bishops' War

- In 1637, Charles and Laud introduced the new Prayer Book to Scotland and tried to give Scottish bishops the same powers as English ones. However, when the Prayer Book was first used in Scotland it led to riots.

- In 1638, the Scots signed a Covenant declaring that they would defend their Protestantism. The following year, Charles sent an army to Scotland to enforce his changes.

- But in the struggle that followed, known as the First Bishops' War, the army was easily defeated by the Scots.

- In 1639, Parliament accused Laud of treason. He was tried in 1644, found guilty and executed the following year.

16.4 Charles I and Parliament

Charles I was already unpopular with many MPs because of his religious beliefs and his insistence on the Divine Right of Kings.

- Charles, like his father, was also a lavish spender. He was also under the influence of the Duke of Buckingham, who was unpopular with Parliament. Buckingham led a disastrous naval raid on the port of Cadiz in Spain and was then murdered by a disgruntled sailor.

- In 1627, in response to being offered only one-tenth of the money he requested, Charles dissolved Parliament. He therefore had to borrow the money from the people in a forced loan.

- In 1628, Charles attempted to increase the tax on certain goods. A group of MPs, led by John Pym, drew up the Petition of Right, which reminded the King that he had no right to raise taxes or take forced loans of his own accord.

- When Parliament presented Charles with the similar Three Resolutions the following year, he dissolved Parliament again. This time it was not called for 11 years, a period known as 'The Eleven Year Tyranny'.

- Charles reintroduced old laws that had been forgotten and fined people for breaking them. He also continued to sell monopolies and titles.

- In 1635, Charles extended the ship money tax to all inland counties as well as coastal counties. An MP named John Hampden refused to pay his ship money, but was tried and forced to pay.

The Short and Long Parliaments (1640)

- After defeat in the First Bishops' War (see page 92), Charles needed to raise a bigger army against the Scots. Thomas Wentworth, the Earl of Strafford, advised the King to call Parliament and ask for the necessary funding. The MPs refused and this 'Short Parliament' was dissolved after three weeks.

- The Second Bishops' War also failed. Charles signed the Treaty of Ripon, in which he agreed to give to Scotland three counties of northern England and £850 per day.

- Charles returned to Parliament asking for more money. In this 'Long Parliament', the MPs, led by John Pym, blamed Strafford for the cost of the defeat and put him on trial for treason. Parliament passed a Bill of Attainder allowing him to be executed in May 1641.

- Charles was forced to agree to a number of other demands from the MPs. Ship money and the sale of monopolies were discontinued. Parliament was allowed to punish the King's ministers and choose their replacements.

- Parliament was also compelled to meet at least every three years and MPs were allowed to vote against the King's attempts to dissolve it. The King's courts that sat without juries, such as the Star Chamber, were abolished.

- The Long Parliament was so-called because it was not officially dissolved until 1660 (see page 102).

✓ Try using index cards to help with the key points on Charles I: one for religion, one for the First Bishops' War, another for Parliament and a fourth for the Short and Long Parliaments. Don't forget to test yourself by writing questions on the front of the card and the answers on the back.

16.5 Causes of the Civil War

With Parliament able to control the King's finances, Charles was becoming powerless to act without their agreement.

Rebellion in Ireland

- Rebellion broke out in Ireland in October 1641. Phelim O'Neill raised a force that killed 12,000 Protestants in Ulster.

- John Pym granted the money to put down the rebellion, on the condition that Parliament chose who would command the army.

The Grand Remonstrance (1641)

- Charles refused Parliament's demand and, in November 1641, Pym submitted the Grand Remonstrance. Pym demanded that Parliament should appoint the King's ministers in future.

- On 4th January 1642, the King entered Parliament with 400 soldiers and called for the arrest of the five most rebellious MPs: John Pym, John Hampden, Arthur Haselrig, Denzil Holles and William Strode. But they had already escaped by boat along the River Thames.

- Charles's actions on that day were in breach of Parliamentary privilege, which stated that no MP could be arrested inside the House of Commons.

- In February 1642, the Puritan MPs again demanded the abolition of bishops. Some MPs who had previously supported Pym and the rebels were now alarmed at the thought of Puritans controlling the country.

The Nineteen Propositions (1642)

- In June 1642, Parliament passed the Nineteen Propositions. These called for the approval of Parliament in all affairs of state and the appointment of all ministers, and the right of Parliament to control the army.

- Puritan MPs had also pushed for laws against Catholics to be enforced and the right of Parliament to dictate how the Church should be reformed.

- Moderate MPs became even more alarmed. Parliament became strongly divided, with many MPs now openly supporting the King.

In August 1642, Charles rode to Nottingham. His royal standard was raised and he called on all his loyal subjects to fight with him against the rebels in Parliament. The English Civil War had begun.

> ✓ Make up a story connecting the events leading to the Civil War to help you remember what happened. Add descriptions to make the characters and events come to life.

Evidence question

You may be asked to answer an evidence question on the causes of the Civil War. Refer to the guidance on pages xi–xii and make sure that you practise answering these questions.

Summary

You should now know the following:

1. The religious views of James I and the events of the Gunpowder Plot.

2. The relationship between James I and Parliament.

3. The religious views of Charles I and the events of the Bishops' Wars with Scotland.

4. The relationship between Charles I and Parliament.

5. The short-term causes of the English Civil War.

Test yourself

Before moving on to the next chapter, make sure you can answer the following questions. The answers are at the back of the book.

1. When and where did James I refuse to dismiss the English bishops?

2. Why was the Addled Parliament of 1614 dissolved after eight weeks?

3. Which unpopular tax led to the trial of John Hampden?

4. Which five MPs did Charles I attempt to arrest in January 1642?

Chapter 17: Civil War (1642–1649) and the Interregnum (1649–1660)

17.1 The English Civil War

The two sides in the English Civil War each formed an army.

- The Royalist army consisted of the old nobility, courtiers, Roman Catholics and Anglicans, and men from the country. They were known as Cavaliers.

- The Parliamentarian army consisted of the lesser gentry, merchants, Puritans and Presbyterians, and men from towns. They were known as Roundheads.

Charles and his army marched south to reclaim London. The Roundheads marched north and the two sides met at Edgehill in Warwickshire.

The key battles of the Civil War

- The Battle of Edgehill was fought on 23rd October 1642. The Cavaliers were commanded by Charles's nephew Prince Rupert of the Rhine.

- The battle lasted three hours and ended in a stalemate, with no clear winner.

- Charles could have pushed on towards London, but he was unsure about whether he would face any resistance there. He therefore decided to wait.

In 1643, both sides won smaller battles but Charles still failed to march on London. Parliament made a pact with Scotland that drew them on to their side.

17.2 The Battle of Marston Moor, 2nd July 1644

- In 1644, Royalist forces in York were being held under siege by the Parliamentarians. Charles sent Prince Rupert to relieve his forces. Rupert managed to free the city and then chased the enemy onto the moors.

- Sir Thomas Fairfax ordered the Parliamentarians to turn around and prepare for battle on Marston Moor, and the Roundheads lined up in formation along a defensive ridge.

- The Cavaliers lined up facing them, with foot soldiers in the centre and cavalry on both sides.

- Many horsemen were undisciplined and would break away from their group to chase a retreating enemy. A Roundhead and Puritan MP named Oliver Cromwell had trained his cavalry division well and these horsemen, known as 'Ironsides', always kept their formation.

- By the evening of 2nd July, Prince Rupert was convinced that there would be no fighting that day and left the field. At this point, the Parliamentarians chose to advance.

- Cromwell's men, on the left flank facing Rupert's division, charged the Royalist cavalry, who retreated.

- Sir Thomas Fairfax's men, on the right flank, were routed by the Cavaliers. But these horsemen were undisciplined and broke ranks, allowing the Roundhead infantry on the right to intercept them.

- Sir Thomas Fairfax found himself behind the Royalist lines and managed to work his way behind them to join up with Cromwell's forces on the left flank. Their horsemen then ploughed into the Royalist foot soldiers, scattering them.

The Battle of Marston Moor

97

- The Cavaliers commanded by the Marquess of Newcastle, known as 'Whitecoats', made a stand against the Parliamentarians, fighting until they were overwhelmed. This allowed many of the Royalists to flee the battlefield safely.

- By the end of the battle, the Royalists had lost 4,000 men and the Parliamentarians had lost 1,000.

17.3 Oliver Cromwell and the New Model Army

Oliver Cromwell encouraged Parliament to set up a permanent army that would always be on hand to fight their cause. This became known as the New Model Army.

- Sir Thomas Fairfax commanded the infantry and Cromwell the cavalry. The soldiers were highly trained and told that they were fighting for God's will.

- The soldiers were given uniforms to wear and were relatively well paid. Cromwell trained his horsemen to keep in formation at all times.

- At the Battle of Naseby in June 1645, their training kept the formation tight and the Cavaliers were eventually forced to retreat.

- As he made to escape, the King's private papers fell into the hands of the Roundheads. They showed that he had been asking for assistance from Ireland and France.

- The following year, Charles was captured by the Scots, who sold him to the Parliamentarians in 1647. The MPs tried to come to an agreement with the King. They wanted Parliament to control the army for ten years, after which time it would revert to the King's control. This offer was refused.

- Charles managed to escape and fled to the Isle of Wight, but he was again captured and locked up in Carisbrooke Castle. From there, he made a secret deal with Scottish Presbyterians. The idea was that they would crush the Parliamentarians and restore Charles to the throne.

- The Scots invaded England but were defeated at the Battle of Preston in August 1648. The Parliamentarians had won the English Civil War.

There were several important reasons for the Parliamentarian victory:

- Charles ran out of money and could not afford to train or equip his soldiers well.

- Parliament controlled the south-east of England, which was the richest area of the country.

- The navy was on Parliament's side, meaning that Charles had difficulty getting foreign soldiers to England.

- Prince Rupert had little experience of how to command the infantry.

- The New Model Army was better trained, better equipped and had more skilful commanders, such as Cromwell and Fairfax.

- Charles never succeeded in regaining London from the Parliamentarians.

- Charles's strategy was often poor, for example he failed to continue his advance to London after the Battle of Edgehill in 1642.

✓ Use a chart with different branches to help you remember the events of the English Civil War. One branch could cover the key battles, another Oliver Cromwell and his army and another branch the reasons for the Parliamentarian victory.

17.4 The trial and execution of Charles I

When Charles was arrested, the MPs debated what should be done with him. Most, like Cromwell, argued that they had tried to negotiate with the King before and that he had re-started the war by involving the Scots.

- On 6th December 1648, the Parliamentarian army surrounded the House of Commons and only allowed entry to those MPs who supported putting the King on trial. This was known as 'Pride's Purge'.

- The 240 MPs who were allowed entry to the House of Commons formed the Rump Parliament. They voted to put Charles on trial. The trial began in January 1649.

There were several charges against the King:

- He had abused his powers as King, ruling as a tyrant.

- He had declared war on his own people.

- He had attempted to turn the French and Irish against his own people.

- He had re-started the war by encouraging the Scots to invade.

✓ You could try making up a phrase to help you remember the charges against Charles or perhaps use an illustration for each charge.

Charles claimed that the court had no right to put him on trial and refused to answer the charges.

- Eighty commissioners took part in the trial of Charles. The King was found guilty by 68 of the judges, 59 of whom signed his death warrant.

- The execution took place on the morning of 30th January 1649.

17.5 Cromwell and Parliament

With the King dead, Parliament declared England to be a Commonwealth. The House of Lords was abolished and a Council of State, consisting of MPs chosen from the Rump Parliament, was introduced. The real power to enforce the laws lay with the army, now commanded by Cromwell.

- The Rump Parliament did not prove to be effective and Cromwell was unable to bring about the reforms he really wanted.

- He dissolved the Rump Parliament on 20th April 1653. In its place, the new assembly became known as Barebone's Parliament. Cromwell wanted this to be a 'Parliament of the Saints' that would make laws according to strictly Puritan values.

- But the various groups in Barebone's Parliament were unable to work together. In December 1653, 40 frustrated MPs marched to Cromwell's home and handed their authority over to him.

- Barebone's Parliament was dissolved and, on 16th December 1653, Cromwell was appointed Lord Protector of England.

Lord Protector

- In 1655, England was divided into 11 districts and a Major-General was appointed in charge of keeping law and order in each one. A ten per cent tax, the decimation tax, was introduced to finance the Major-General's local armies in each district.

- Cromwell banned unlawful assemblies and the owning of weapons by known Royalists, and called for robbers and vagrants to be severely punished.

- While people were free to worship as they wished in private, new laws were introduced that attempted to make their way of life as Puritan as possible. Entertainment, dancing, singing and drinking alcohol were banned, as was the celebration of Christmas.

- In 1657, Cromwell gathered together his army leaders to discuss the drawing-up of a new constitution for England. The men were adamant that Cromwell should not declare himself a replacement for the monarch they had got rid of.

- Nonetheless, later that year, Cromwell was formally sworn in as Lord Protector in a magnificent ceremony, full of pomp and splendour that showed off his power.

Sample question

Try this sample essay question for yourself. A suggested answer is given at the back of the book.

Q.   (a) Describe the main events of Oliver Cromwell's rule as Lord Protector.   (20)

   (b) Explain why there might have been opposition to the ceremony appointing
       Cromwell as Lord Protector in 1657.   (10)

17.6 Ireland and Scotland

Ireland and Scotland had been ruled by the kings of England for many years. Now that the monarchy had been abolished, they declared themselves independent.

The conquest of Ireland

- Parliament feared that Charles I's son, also named Charles, might seek Irish support for his restoration to the throne.

- In 1649, Cromwell led a force to Ireland, occupied Dublin and attacked the town of Drogheda, killing around 3,500 Irish. In the southern town of Wexford, a further 1,500 Irish were killed in a similar assault.

- The Parliamentarians forced the Catholics to resettle in Connaught, in the west of Ireland. The lands that they left were divided up between Cromwell's men.

The conquest of Scotland

- In Scotland, Charles I's son (Charles Stuart) had been accepted as monarch and crowned King Charles II. This time, his supporters were not Catholics but Presbyterians.

- A Parliamentarian army defeated the Scots in battle at Dunbar in September 1650 and captured the city of Edinburgh.

- The Scottish forces, with Charles, moved south into England. In September 1651, the two sides fought a street battle in the city of Worcester, which the Parliamentarians won.

- Charles escaped and, according to legend, hid from Cromwell's men in an oak tree. He then crossed over to France.

✓ You could use a flow chart to help you remember what happened in Ireland and Scotland. Use two rows, one for Ireland and one for Scotland, and use a different bubble for each of the key points. Think how you might finish the one below.

Ireland and Scotland after Civil War

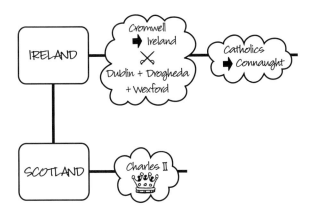

101

17.7 Richard Cromwell and the Restoration

Oliver Cromwell died on 3rd September 1658. His son Richard had been named as his father's successor by the 1657 constitution.

- Richard Cromwell had not been a soldier and did not have any military experience. He therefore could not depend on the support of the army.

- He was forced to call Parliament and ask for taxes to be raised to fund the army. Parliament, however, did not want the power of the army to grow and refused.

- With the army and Parliament standing against both him and each other, Richard Cromwell resigned the Protectorate in May 1659.

The return of Charles Stuart

- General George Monck, who commanded the army in Scotland, decided to march south and sort out the situation.

- Monck recalled the Long Parliament, which had not officially been dissolved (see page 93). Parliament agreed that to avoid another civil war, the people had to be united around one man.

- Monck began to negotiate with Charles Stuart and, in April 1660, the Declaration of Breda was signed. Charles would allow a free Parliament, fair wages for soldiers and pardons for those who had fought against his father in the English Civil War. He also agreed to accept the limits placed on the Crown in 1641.

- In May 1660, Parliament declared Charles to be the rightful King.

Summary

You should now know the following:

1.   The key events of the English Civil War and the reasons for the Royalist defeat.

2.   The events of the Battle of Marston Moor in 1644.

3.   The contribution of Oliver Cromwell and the New Model Army to the Parliamentarian victory.

4.   The events and significance of the trial and execution of Charles I.

5.   The relationship between Oliver Cromwell and Parliament, and the events of his rule as Lord Protector.

6.   The events of Oliver Cromwell's conquests of Ireland and Scotland.

7.   The reasons for, and events of, the resignation of Richard Cromwell and the restoration of Charles II.

Test yourself

Before moving on to the next chapter, make sure you can answer the following questions. The answers are at the back of the book.

1. When was the Battle of Edgehill?

2. Which Royalist commanded the 'Whitecoats' at the Battle of Marston Moor?

3. With whom did Charles I make secret negotiations while imprisoned in Carisbrooke Castle?

4. Which tax financed the local armies of the 11 Major-Generals?

5. How is Charles II supposed to have escaped capture by Cromwell's forces after the Battle of Worcester in 1651?

6. By which document did Charles II agree to the terms of his restoration to the throne?

Chapter 18: Charles II (1660–1685) and James II (1685–1688)

18.1 Charles II

Charles II, known as the 'Merrie Monarch', was exactly the sort of king the Puritans hoped would never return to England.

- Charles lived well and spent lavishly. He is best known for his many mistresses, including the actress Nell Gwynn, and for fathering many illegitimate children.

- Although he had agreed to pardon those who had fought on the Parliamentarian side, Charles was determined to punish those involved in the death of his father. The surviving commissioners who had sentenced Charles I to death were put on trial for regicide and either imprisoned or executed.

- The corpses of some Republican figures who had already died – including Oliver Cromwell himself – were exhumed, publicly hanged and then decapitated. Their heads were placed upon poles.

- The Parliament that elected to restore Charles to the throne was called the Convention Parliament. It repealed all the Acts of Parliament passed during the *interregnum*.

- The next session, the Cavalier Parliament, allowed the King to regain some of the rights that had been taken from his father.

- Charles regained control of the army and Parliament agreed to give the army a sum of money every year to support it.

- Later, the members of the Cavalier Parliament began to split into two groups. One group – the Tory Party – was strongly supportive of the King. The other – the Whig Party – wanted to restrict the King's power.

18.2 Plague and fire

The Great Plague (1665)

- In 1665, bubonic plague returned to England and took hold in London.

- A member of the King's government named Samuel Pepys kept a diary during the years 1660–1669. It is a valuable source of information on the effects of the outbreak on the people of London.

- People living in infected houses were quarantined for a month under the guard of watchmen. The infected

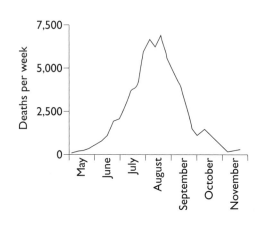

houses were marked with a red cross. Women were employed to keep track of the deaths and record the number of victims.

- The number of deaths in London peaked during August, when the weather was hottest. As it grew colder, the rate of victims dropped, and Charles returned to London in February 1666.

Evidence question

You may be asked to answer an evidence question on the 1665 Plague of London. Refer to the guidance on pages xi–xii and make sure that you practise answering these questions.

The Great Fire of London (1666)

- In the early hours of 2nd September 1666, a fire broke out in Thomas Farynor's bakery in Pudding Lane. It quickly spread through the neighbouring wooden houses.

- Fanned by strong easterly winds that drove the flames westwards, the fire lasted five days.

- There were very few human casualties, but the fire engulfed three-quarters of the land within the city walls. Thousands of people were made homeless or lost their trade.

- When the city was rebuilt, the streets were made wider and buildings were constructed with brick and stone rather than wood. Sir Christopher Wren designed the new St Paul's Cathedral and a monument to the fire that stands close to where Pudding Lane once was.

18.3 Charles II and religion

Charles was keen to solve the issue of religion once and for all. He wanted to strengthen the authority of the Church and passed a series of four Acts of Parliament known as the Clarendon Code.

The Clarendon Code

- The Corporation Act (1661) banned non-conformists from holding public office and forced officials to be members of the Church of England.

- The Act of Uniformity (1662) made the use of the *Book of Common Prayer* compulsory in church services.

- The Coventicle Act (1664) banned coventicles, which were unauthorised meetings for worship.

- The Five-Mile Act (1665) banned non-conformist ministers from coming within five miles of their former parishes or teaching in schools.

Think up a phrase, using the first letters of each of the Acts, to help you remember the order in which they were passed:

Corporation Act (1661)	C
Act of **U**niformity (1662)	U
Coventicle Act (1664)	C
Five-Mile Act (1665)	F

The Popish Plot (1678)

- Charles was sympathetic to Catholicism and, in 1672, he drew up a Declaration of Indulgence, allowing greater freedom of worship to those who were not members of the Church of England.

- The mostly Protestant MPs did not want to give Catholics any more freedom. They passed the Test Act (1673), which forced government ministers to swear an oath against the key Catholic belief of transubstantiation.

- Charles's brother James married the Catholic Mary of Modena in 1673, after the death of his first wife Anne Hyde.

- In 1678, an Anglican priest named Titus Oates claimed that Mary of Modena and several important Catholics were plotting to assassinate Charles and place James on the throne.

- The Whigs attempted to pass the Exclusion Bill, which would have made Charles's illegitimate son James Scott, the Protestant Duke of Monmouth, heir to the throne instead.

- The Bill was blocked by the House of Lords, but in the meantime anti-Catholic riots had led to the arrest and trial of several Catholics who were imprisoned or executed for treason.

- Titus Oates's story was untrue and he was found guilty of perjury. Despite this, much of the anti-Catholic feeling remained, with Catholics being persecuted and banned from holding public office.

Charles's brother James remained under suspicion until the Rye House Plot of 1683, when certain Whig MPs were found to be plotting the murder of both him and the King. The discovery of the plot caused a great deal of public sympathy towards James, who was allowed to succeed to the throne on the death of his brother in February 1685. Charles converted to Catholicism on his deathbed.

18.4 James II and the Monmouth Rebellion

Almost immediately, James faced a dangerous rebellion by the Duke of Monmouth.

- Monmouth claimed to have legal papers proving that his parents were in fact married and that he was therefore legitimate. His claim was supported by those who wanted a Protestant king.

- Monmouth marched through the West Country attempting to gain support, but he was only able to gather a relatively small army of 6,000 men.

- The royal army met Monmouth at the Battle of Sedgemoor on 6th July 1685. The rebels were soundly defeated and Monmouth was captured and untidily beheaded a week later.

- James appointed Lord Chief Justice Jeffreys to preside over the trials of the remaining rebels. These court sessions became known as the Bloody Assizes, with 300 prisoners being executed.

- After the rebellion, James requested Parliament's support for a standing army, with Catholics commanding several of the regiments.

- When his request was refused, James dissolved Parliament in November 1685 and never called another session.

18.5 The Glorious Revolution

As a Catholic, James was keen to continue his brother's reforms, despite the objections of many.

- Catholics were appointed to important government positions. In 1687, a church court was set up to dismiss any Anglican clerics who were critical of this.

- In the same year, James issued a Declaration of Indulgence that attempted to remove all anti-Catholic laws. When he demanded that it be read out in every church, William Sancroft, the Archbishop of Canterbury, refused, along with six other bishops.

- The churchmen were arrested and put on trial, but were found not guilty. It was the first time a King of England had lost a court case.

- The Dutch ruler, William of Orange, was married to Mary, the eldest daughter of James II and his first wife Anne Hyde. Both were Protestant and several MPs invited them to England to claim the throne from James.

- James's second wife Mary of Modena gave birth to James Edward Stuart in June 1688. He became the Catholic heir to the throne. It was rumoured that the baby was not a royal prince at all but had actually been smuggled into the palace in a warming pan.

- William of Orange sailed to England with 15,000 Dutch and English soldiers, landing at Brixham in Devon on 5th November 1688.

- James fled to France the following month. The crown was offered to Mary as James's daughter, but William refused to allow this unless he could rule jointly with his wife. They were crowned King William III and Queen Mary II in April 1689.

✓ Try using a sketch or, perhaps, a flow chart to help you remember the events of the Glorious Revolution. Remember to use different colours to help you remember the different points.

Evidence question

You may be asked to answer an evidence question on James II and the Glorious Revolution. Refer to the guidance on pages xi–xii and make sure that you practise answering these questions.

18.6 Culture and science

The reigns of the Tudors and Stuarts brought great advances in the arts and science. Many famous artists, writers, scientists and philosophers of the period produced works that are still studied and enjoyed today.

Artists

- Hans Holbein (c.1497–1543) was the most important court painter of his time, producing famous portraits of Henry VIII and Edward VI.

- Nicholas Hilliard (c.1547–1619) was a specialist in producing miniatures.

- Anthony van Dyck (1599–1641) was the main court painter during the reign of Charles I.

Writers

- William Shakespeare (1564–1616) was the most famous and influential playwright of his age, and 38 of his plays survive today. Shakespeare and a group of players called the King's Men built their own theatre called the Globe.

- Edmund Spenser (1552–1599) is regarded as one of the greatest English poets. He was particularly popular with Elizabeth I and wrote an allegory, *The Faerie Queene*, in her honour.

- Christopher Marlowe (1564–1593) was a playwright as popular as Shakespeare during his lifetime, but died young after a drunken brawl in a tavern.

- John Bunyan (1628–1688) was a non-conformist who was imprisoned for preaching without a licence. While in prison, he wrote a famous allegory called *The Pilgrim's Progress*.

Scientists

- Francis Bacon (1561–1626) encouraged the empirical method, which argued that scientific knowledge was gained by the observation of behaviour rather than the discussion of possible theories.

- William Harvey (1578–1657) discovered the method of circulation by which blood is pumped around the body.

- In 1660 Charles II set up the Royal Society, which provided a place for scientists to carry out their work without fear of attack by the Church. The following scientists were all members of the Society.

- Isaac Newton (1642–1727) is known as the founder of modern science. He famously studied gravity and drew up several laws of motion.

- Christopher Wren (1632–1723) was an architect who rebuilt London after the Great Fire of 1666.

- Edmond Halley (1656–1742) was an astronomer who discovered Halley's Comet and helped to map much of the universe that is visible from Earth.

✓ You could use pictures to help you remember what each of the scientists contributed. Think what you would draw for each of the table entries.

Francis Bacon	
William Harvey	
Isaac Newton	
Christopher Wren	
Edmond Halley	

Philosophers

- Thomas Hobbes (1588–1679) argued that people are naturally wicked and unfit to hold positions of authority. He therefore believed that monarchy was the best form of government.

- John Locke (1632–1704) argued that people are born as a 'blank slate' (*tabula rasa*) without ideas, and that their experiences in life form their way of thinking. He did not support the idea of monarchy.

Summary

You should now know the following:

1.   The early events of the reign of Charles II.

2.   The events of the Great Plague of 1665 and the Great Fire of London of 1666.

3.   The religious views of Charles II, and the events and consequences of the Popish Plot.

4.   The early events of the reign of James II and the Monmouth Rebellion.

5.   The religious views of James II, and the events and consequences of the Glorious Revolution.

6.   The work of the most famous artists, writers, scientists and philosophers of the period.

Test yourself

Before moving on to the next chapter, make sure you can answer the following questions. The answers are at the back of the book.

1.   Which session of Parliament overturned all the laws passed during the *Interregnum*?

2.   Where did the Great Fire of London start?

3.   To which religion did Charles II convert on his deathbed?

4.   At which battle was the Monmouth Rebellion put down?

5.   Where did William of Orange land in November 1688?

Chapter 19: William III and Mary II (1689–1702) and Anne (1702–1714)

19.1 William III and Mary II

William III and Mary II were crowned King and Queen of England at the request of Parliament, but they had to agree to certain conditions.

- The Bill of Rights (1689) allowed only Protestants to inherit the throne. The monarch could not have a standing army during peacetime and could not impose taxes without the approval of Parliament.

- The Toleration Act (1689) allowed people to worship in private as they wished, but Catholics and dissenters were still banned from holding positions of authority.

- The Triennial Act (1694) required Parliament to be called every three years. Parliament had to have access to the royal accounts. In return, it would grant the monarchy a sum of money each year called the Civil List.

Think up a phrase, using the first letter of each of the Acts, to help you remember them:

Bill of **R**ights (1689)   R

Toleration Act (1689)   T

Triennial Act (1694)   T

How about: a right tolerant trifle!

19.2 Ireland and France

After James II fled to France following the Glorious Revolution, he was offered support by King Louis XIV of France. Louis helped James to raise an army, which then sailed to Ireland.

- James was welcomed by the Irish Catholics. His army marched into Protestant Ulster and besieged the city of Derry.

- The siege lasted for more than three months and caused the deaths of thousands of Protestants. It was finally broken when William's navy managed to break into the harbour and land.

- William and James met at the Battle of the Boyne on 12th July 1690. James was soundly defeated and returned to France.

- After Mary died in 1694, William turned his attention to Louis XIV. His navy defeated the French at the Battles of Barfleur and La Hogue. Louis was forced to make peace with William in 1697.

19.3 The Act of Settlement (1701)

William and Mary had no children, so it seemed that the throne might pass to Mary's closest male relative, her Catholic half-brother James Edward Stuart.

- Parliament drew up the Act of Settlement, which formally banned a Catholic, or anyone who married a Catholic, from ever inheriting the throne.

- The Act also named Mary's sister Anne as the heir to the throne and declared that on her death, the Crown would pass to James I's granddaughter Sophia of Hanover and her descendants. This is known as the Hanoverian succession (see page 115).

- William III died in March 1702 and, according to the terms of the Act, was succeeded by Anne.

19.4 Anne and war with France

When Anne came to the throne, France and Spain had been at war for some years.

- In 1699, the kingdom of Spain had been left to Philip of Anjou, the grandson of Louis XIV of France. Louis now claimed Spain, and also threatened Holland and Austria.

- In 1702, England declared war on France. Prussia, Denmark and Holland joined England's side in what became known as the War of the Spanish Succession.

- In 1704, John Churchill, the Duke of Marlborough, marched an army of 56,000 men 300 miles across Europe. The army consisted of Englishmen and Germans led by Prince Eugene of Savoy.

- The allied forces met a French and Bavarian army, commanded by Marshal Tallard, outside the village of Blenheim on 13th August 1704.

> ✓ You could also try thinking up a phrase to help you remember the events and people involved in the war with France:
>
> | | |
> |---|---|
> | **L**ouis XIV | L |
> | John **C**hurchill | C |
> | Prince **E**ugene | E |
> | Marshal **T**allard | T |

19.5 The Battle of Blenheim, 13th August 1704

● The two armies lined up for battle on either side of a stream called the Nebel. Tallard was confident that if anyone tried to cross this, the Franco-Bavarian cavalry could quickly charge them.

● Marlborough knew that his cavalry were stronger. Tallard had arranged a large group of cavalry in the centre, with more infantry on both flanks. Marlborough planned to attack the two flanks at once, keeping them occupied while pushing a large force of cavalry through the weaker centre.

● Lord Cutts on the eastern flank and Prince Eugene on the western flank both managed to keep the enemy occupied.

● Marlborough's cavalry marched across the Nebel in the centre. The French cavalry charged in small groups, coming under attack by fire from the English infantry.

● As the allied forces pushed forward, the French cavalry in the centre broke position and ran. The battle resulted in nearly 40,000 French and Bavarian soldiers being killed or captured, in contrast to 6,000 English and German dead.

● Marlborough fought and won several more victories and France finally signed the Peace of Utrecht in 1713. France now promised to stop supporting the claims of James Edward Stuart. It also gave up some valuable colonies to England.

The Battle of Blenheim

	British and Allied foot soldiers		French and Bavarian foot soldiers
	British and Allied cavalry		French and Bavarian cavalry
▲▲▲	British and Allied artillery	▲▲▲	French and Bavarian artillery

19.6 The Act of Union (1707)

- The Act of Settlement was not popular in Scotland. The Scots wanted the right to choose their own monarch and they preferred James Edward Stuart.

- Scotland had not supported England during the war with France and Anne's government was worried that the two countries would form an alliance.

- It was suggested that the English and Scottish Parliaments be merged, so that the two sides could debate the issue. The English promised a sum of money to Scottish merchants who had lost business as a result of English trading activities.

- The Act of Union was finally agreed in May 1707, and the two Parliaments were united, with Anne as Queen of Great Britain. Scotland kept its own Church, but everything else was shared with England.

Sample question

Try this sample essay question for yourself. A suggested answer is given at the back of the book.

Q.   (a) Describe the events leading to the Act of Union in 1707. (20)

   (b) Explain why there was both opposition and support for this Act in Scotland. (10)

Summary

You should now know the following:

1.   The Acts of Parliament establishing the positions of William III and Mary II on the throne.

2.   The events of the Irish and French attempts to restore James II.

3.   The provisions and consequences of the Act of Settlement (1701).

4.   The events of the War of the Spanish Succession and the Battle of Blenheim in 1704.

5.   The provisions and consequences of the Act of Union (1707).

Test yourself

Before moving on to the next chapter, make sure you can answer the following questions. The answers are at the back of the book.

1.   What was allowed by the Toleration Act (1689)?

2.   When was the Battle of the Boyne?

3.   Who led the German allies at the Battle of Blenheim?

4.   Which treaty ended the fighting between Britain and France in 1713?

5.   When did the Act of Union come into effect?

Chapter 20: George I (1714–1727) and George II (1727–1760)

20.1 George I and the 1715 Jacobite Rebellion

Anne died in August 1714 and, according to the Act of Settlement, the crown passed to the House of Hanover. As Sophia of Hanover had died only a few months previously, the throne passed to her son, who became George I. Almost immediately, he faced a rebellion from those who wanted James Edward Stuart (the 'Old Pretender') on the throne.

- The supporters of James Edward Stuart were known as Jacobites. The Earl of Mar declared James King in 1715. He raised a rebel army of around 10,000 men, which was severely defeated by a government force at the Battle of Sheriffmuir in November.

- Another Jacobite force was defeated at Preston and James returned to exile in France in February 1716.

- There was still Jacobite support in the Highlands and the government set up a series of forts – Fort William, Fort Augustus and Fort George – from which it intended to put down any future uprisings.

> ✓ You could try using word and picture links to help you remember the forts that were set up in the Highlands. Use blank playing cards with the picture on the front and the name of the fort on the back. See *Study Skills*, pages 64 and 65 for help with this.

20.2 Parliament and Walpole

The two political parties – the Whigs and the Tories – continued to develop during the reign of George I.

- Some Tories were known to be sympathetic to the Jacobites. George therefore aligned himself with the Whigs.

- George formed a Regency Council to run the country while he was in Hanover and this Council met in a room called the Cabinet.

- The Cabinet meetings were chaired by a senior minister who reported to the King. From 1721, this senior minister was the First Lord of the Treasury, Robert Walpole, who is today regarded as Britain's first Prime Minister.

- During this period, Britain was heavily in debt and the South Sea Company had been granted a monopoly in return for lending more money to clear the foreign debts.

- In 1720, the company ran into difficulty and the price of shares plummeted. Millions of pounds were lost.

- Walpole found that the company had exaggerated the prospect of gaining money to its shareholders. Those found guilty of corruption were imprisoned.

- In 1722, a Jacobite plot was discovered in which Francis Atterbury, a leading Tory, was implicated. Walpole convinced people that all Tories were Jacobite rebels and the Whigs became more popular.

20.3 Trade and the empire

During the reign of George I, Britain's trade routes across the world became established.

Britain's Empire at the time of George I

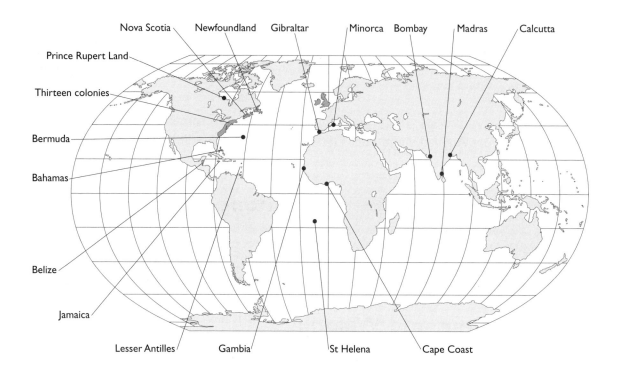

- By 1727, Britain owned colonies in America, the West Indies and parts of Canada. There were also trading bases in India and Gibraltar.

- Trade routes between Britain, Africa and America formed a system called the Triangular Trade. The British took manufactured goods to Africa and sold them in exchange for slaves. The slaves were then transported to America and exchanged for valuable commodities, such as tobacco, cotton, sugar and coffee, which were then shipped back to Britain.

The Triangular Trade

Produce to Europe

Sugar
Tobacco
Cotton
Coffee
to Europe

Alcohol
Horses
Guns
Pots
to Africa

Slaves
to the Americas

Goods to Africa

Slaves to the West Indies

George I died while on a visit to Hanover in June 1727. He was succeeded by his son, who became George II.

20.4 George II and war with Europe

The War of Jenkins' Ear (1739–1742)

● British success in gaining an empire had been greatly resented by Spain. In 1729, Spain signed the Treaty of Seville, which gave Spaniards the right to board British ships sailing in Spanish waters.

● In 1731, Spaniards boarded a British ship captained by Robert Jenkins, who had his ear cut off in the ensuing fight.

● Several years later, Jenkins displayed his preserved ear to Parliament and the outrage it caused led to war being declared on Spain.

● The following year, the British captured the Spanish town of Porto Bello in Panama, but any further attempts to take Spanish strongholds failed. Robert Walpole was forced to resign in 1742.

The War of the Austrian Succession (1742–1748)

● In 1740, the Emperor of Austria, Charles VI, died and left the throne to his daughter Maria Theresa. This succession was disputed by Frederick II of Prussia.

● Prussia was supported by France, who threatened to invade Hanover in 1742, bringing George – and Britain – into the conflict. George personally led an army of English and Hanoverians at the Battle of Dettingen on 27th June 1743 and defeated the French.

- France then raided the British fortified towns in Maine in 1745. A combined force of British and American colonials captured the French fortification of Fort Louisbourg in Nova Scotia.

- Both sides signed the Treaty of Aix-la-Chapelle in 1748, ending the war.

20.5 The 1745 Jacobite Rebellion

By 1745, James Edward Stuart had a 24-year-old son, Charles, who was to enter folk legend as Bonnie Prince Charlie.

- Charles landed with a small group of followers on the island of Eriksay, off the west coast of Scotland, in July 1745. He gained the support of several Scottish clans, raising an army of over 4,000.

- The Jacobites defeated a government army at the Battle of Prestonpans on 21st September 1745.

- Charles crossed the border into England, confident that English Jacobites would support him. But this did not happen and, by the time they reached Derby, Charles's advisors persuaded him to turn back.

- Back in Scotland, Charles tried to capture Stirling Castle. The Jacobites managed to defeat another government army at the Battle of Falkirk on 17th January 1746.

- George II asked his son William, Duke of Cumberland, to go after the Jacobites. The two sides met on Culloden Moor, near Inverness, on 16th April 1746.

The Battle of Culloden, 16th April 1746

- The Jacobites were short of food and supplies, and expected reinforcements from France which had not yet arrived.

- Charles and his highest commander, Lord George Murray, disagreed over when and where to fight. Charles refused to listen to Murray's advice to withdraw from Culloden and fight elsewhere.

The Battle of Culloden

- The government army formed two lines with the cavalry placed on each flank. The Jacobites placed the Highlanders in the front line.

- The government army's cannon were more accurate and caused more damage than the Jacobite guns.

- The Highlanders on the right flank charged toward the government army. Cumberland's men opened fire with their muskets and cannon loaded with grapeshot.

- The charging Highlanders were slaughtered by the well-trained government soldiers, who used their bayonets to spear as the enemy raised their sword arms.

- Charles and the Jacobites retreated. Around 1,000 Jacobites were lost, compared with only 50 government soldiers.

- For the next three months, Cumberland's troops rounded up 3,500 men and executed more than 100.

- Charles escaped to the Isle of Skye, with the help of a local girl named Flora Macdonald. He reached France and lived in exile for the rest of his life.

Sample question

Try this sample essay question for yourself. A suggested answer is given at the back of the book.

Q. (a) Describe the main events of the 1745 Jacobite Rebellion. (20)

(b) Explain why the Rebellion was not successful. (10)

Evidence question

You may be asked to answer an evidence question on the 1745 Jacobite Rebellion. Refer to the guidance on pages xi–xii and make sure that you practise answering these questions.

Summary

You should now know the following:

1. The events and consequences of the 1715 Jacobite Rebellion.

2. The development of the political party system and position of Robert Walpole during the reign of George I.

3. The reasons for the establishment and growth of the British Empire.

4. The events of the War of Jenkins' Ear and the War of the Austrian Succession.

5. The events and consequences of the 1745 Jacobite Rebellion.

Test yourself

Make sure you can answer the following questions. The answers are at the back of the book.

1. Which three government forts were built in Scotland after the 1715 Jacobite Rebellion?

2. Sales of shares in which company caused a stock market crash in 1720?

3. By which treaty were the Spanish allowed to board British vessels in Spanish waters?

4. Who led the English and Hanoverian army at the Battle of Dettingen?

5. Which Jacobite commander advised Bonnie Prince Charlie not to fight at Culloden?

Part C: Britain 1750–c.1900

Chapter 21: The Seven Years' War

21.1 Background

- By 1750, significant communities of British settlers existed on the eastern side of what is now the United States of America. The French had made settlements north of this in what is now Canada.

- In the early 1750s, the French tried to expand their settlements southwards and westwards, into the British colonies of Virginia, New York and Georgia, and built a row of forts along the Appalachian Mountains.

- In 1754, George Washington, a young officer in the Virginia militia, attempted to capture Fort Duquesne from the French, but was defeated. This incident provoked war between the two nations, and both Britain and France sent troops to the colonies to reinforce their armies there.

- In 1755, General Edward Braddock made another attempt to capture Fort Duquesne with more than 2,000 men. But Braddock had no experience of fighting in dense forests. The British were ambushed and defeated by the French and a tribe of Native Americans at the Battle of Monongahela River.

North America and the Seven Years' War

Sample question

Try this sample essay question for yourself. A suggested answer is given at the back of the book.

Q. (a) Describe the events in America between 1750 and 1755. (20)

(b) Explain the reasons why these events led to the outbreak of war. (10)

21.2 William Pitt the Elder

- William Pitt was a Member of Parliament who opposed the Duke of Newcastle's government and the way they were conducting the war. He gained support from his fellow MPs and, despite the refusal of King George II to appoint him Prime Minister, became Secretary of State in 1757 and was placed in charge of the British campaign.

- Pitt believed that the navy was crucial to victory. Under the command of Admiral George Anson the navy blockaded ports in France, preventing their ships from supplying French troops in the colonies.

- Pitt also believed that the French needed to be defeated in the colonies rather than in Europe. However, he gave money to King Frederick the Great of Prussia, encouraging him to keep fighting the French at home.

- Meanwhile, in the colonies, the French captured the British Fort William Henry. Despite French promises to allow the British troops to leave peacefully, 300 soldiers were attacked and killed by their Native American allies.

- The British were outraged by this incident and formed a well-trained brigade of light infantry to launch an offensive against the French. They managed to capture the French forts one by one. Fort Duquesne was destroyed and the site renamed Fort Pitt.

21.3 Wolfe and the fall of Quebec

- Major-General James Wolfe had proved his expertise with nearly 20 years' service in the army. He was popular, with an excellent reputation, but his radical ideas were regarded with suspicion by some. Pitt instructed him to take the city of Quebec, the capital of French Canada.

- Quebec was built at the top of a steep cliff and defended by General Montcalm with 16,000 men. Wolfe had fewer than 10,000 but was supported by a huge navy. These ships sailed up the St Lawrence River in June 1759 and set their guns on Quebec.

- The French planned to hold out until the river froze in the winter. But, on the night of 12th September, Wolfe led a small band of men up the cliffside, overpowering the French militia at the top. The path was cleared for the rest of Wolfe's army to follow.

- The Battle of the Plains of Abraham was fought the next day. Both commanders, Wolfe and Montcalm, were killed, along with 58 British and 500 French troops. The French were routed and forced back into the city of Quebec, which fell to the British five days later.

Map of Quebec showing the sequence of events during the siege

123

21.4 British victories and the end of the campaign

● In the winter of 1760 the French, seeing that the frozen St Lawrence River had forced the British fleet to leave, attempted to retake Quebec. The British managed to hold out until the spring, when the river thawed and their ships were able to return.

● In September 1760, the French surrendered the city of Montreal to General Amherst. The French now no longer had a foothold in Canada.

● The British divided up the old French Canada into smaller colonies and took over the French-owned lands in the West Indies.

● King George II died in October 1760. His grandson, now George III, wanted to end the war, and began to take greater control of the government.

● Pitt resigned as Secretary of State when he could not persuade the government to launch a surprise attack on Spain, which was threatening to join the war, in 1761. Spain did join the war the following year but Britain was able to seize its colonies in Cuba and the Philippines.

● The war ended and a peace treaty, the Peace of Paris, was agreed in 1763. Britain kept control of Canada, but many of the West Indies islands were returned to France. Cuba and the Philippines were returned to Spain, but Britain took control of Florida.

✔ Flash cards are good for testing your knowledge about the important generals and politicians in the Seven Years' War. For example, draw the face of William Pitt (or just his name if you prefer) on one side of a card; on the other side write down his characteristics, accomplishments and failures. See how many of the key points you can remember just from looking at the face side of each card.

You might ask a friend to test you with the flash cards to make it more interesting.

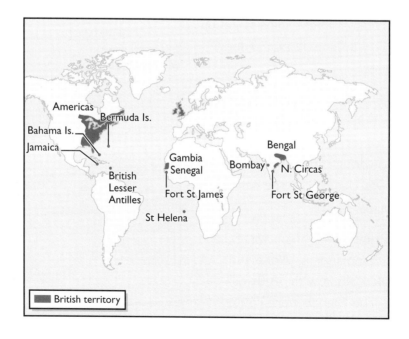

Americas
Bermuda Is.
Bahama Is.
Jamaica
British Lesser Antilles
Gambia
Senegal
Fort St James
St Helena
Bombay
Bengal
N. Circas
Fort St George

█ British territory

Summary

You should now know the following:

1. The events forming the background to the Seven Years' War.

2. The key events in the career of William Pitt the Elder.

3. The reasons for Wolfe's victory and the events of the fall of Quebec.

4. The events surrounding the end of the Seven Years' War.

Test yourself

Before moving on to the next chapter, make sure you can answer the following questions. The answers are at the back of the book.

1. Two attempts were made to capture which French fort in 1754 and 1755?

2. Which European monarch did Pitt the Elder encourage to fight the French in Europe?

3. Who was the French commander during the Battle of the Plains of Abraham?

4. Which peace treaty ended the Seven Years' War in 1763?

Chapter 22: The American Rebellion and World War

22.1 Background

The Seven Years' War placed Britain in £140 million worth of debt. It was decided that its colonies should take their fair share of the burden in paying it off.

The Stamp Tax

- The Stamp Tax was introduced in 1765. Legal documents, newspapers, playing cards and dice now had to bear a stamp that could only be bought from the government.

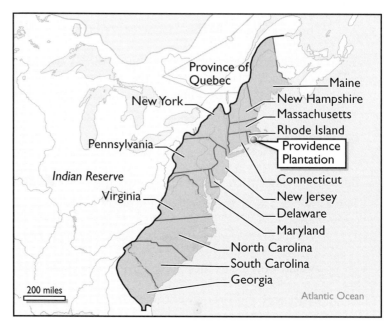

The American colonies in 1770

- A rebel group from Boston, Massachusetts, called the Sons of Liberty, used threats of violence against anyone trying to sell the stamps. They called for a boycott of British goods, at a time when the government had banned the colonies from importing from anywhere else. The trade in goods smuggled in from France and Spain began to grow.

- The rebels declared that the people could only be represented by those they had themselves chosen, and no taxes could be imposed upon them from outside their own colony. They took up the slogan 'No taxation without representation'.

- These protests forced the government to repeal the Stamp Tax in 1766.

The Boston Massacre

- In 1767, the Chancellor of the Exchequer, Charles Townshend, passed the Townshend Duties, a set of taxes on certain goods such as tea, glass, paper and paint.

- A Boston rebel named Samuel Adams persuaded the Massachusetts Assembly to declare the Townshend Duties illegal. The British then sent troops to enforce the taxes. Those who supported Adams called themselves 'Patriots', while those on the British side were termed 'Loyalists'.

- On the night of 5th March 1770, a group of Boston locals were taunting the British soldiers guarding the Customs House. A shot was fired and the soldiers, believing they were under attack, fired into the crowd. In all, five were killed and several more injured.

- Despite the soldiers being found not guilty of murder, the Patriots used the incident to stir up more anti-British feeling.

The Boston Tea Party

- The Townshend Duties were eventually repealed until the only tax remaining was on the import of tea.

- In order to support the East India Company, which was in financial trouble, in 1773 the government decided to sell tea to the colonies at vastly reduced prices. This was both to help the company and to allow the government to collect the import tax as well.

- The Patriots were naturally opposed to this last remaining tax. On the night of 16th December 1773, about 200 Patriots, disguised as Native Americans, went to Boston Harbour and boarded three ships with cargoes of tea waiting to be unloaded. The crates of tea were smashed and the contents thrown over the side.

- The government's reaction was to pass the Coercive Acts the following year. These laws closed the port of Boston, reduced the power of the colonial assembly there, and placed Massachusetts under the military control of General Gage.

- Representatives of Patriots from each colony met at the Continental Congress in September 1774. They agreed to boycott British goods and petitioned King George III with a list of complaints, which was ignored.

22.2 The outbreak of war

General Gage did not expect the militia in Massachusetts to give up easily, and made plans to capture their arms store at Concord.

The Battles of Lexington and Concord

- British soldiers, led by Major Pitcairn, arrived in Lexington at dawn on 19th April 1775, to find a group of armed militiamen parading on the village green. Pitcairn ordered the men to lay down their weapons and disperse, which some attempted to do.

- Then a shot was fired, possibly from the local tavern. The British fired two volleys at the militia and then charged forward with their bayonets. Eight militiamen were killed and ten wounded.

- The British marched on to Concord, where they destroyed the rebels' arms store and set fire to some buildings. Four hundred militiamen began to fire on the British, forcing them back along the road towards Lexington.

- The Patriots dispersed at Lexington when British reinforcements arrived. Forty-nine militiamen were killed; the British lost 73 men and many more were wounded.

The Battle of Bunker Hill

- Once the British had got back to Boston, thousands of militiamen had surrounded the city, digging trenches and trapping General Gage's forces inside.

- On 17th June 1775, the British began to bomb the trenches and earthworks on nearby Bunker Hill, at the entrance to the Charlestown Peninsula. They were commanded by General William Howe.

- The British took three attempts, but eventually managed to overrun the rebel defences and secure the peninsula. However, they suffered heavy losses: over 200 killed and 800 injured.

The British attack on the American position on Breed's Hill; the American rebels were threatening British shipping in the harbour

George Washington and the British

- The Patriots held another Continental Congress in May 1775, at which George Washington was named as the commander of the forces surrounding Boston.

- Washington was an experienced militiaman, and was well liked and respected. He was not a great military tactician but was able to organise supplies and reinforcements to keep his army going, even through the toughest times.

- The colonies rarely agreed on anything and had no established system of government, or a professional army. It was thought that Britain, with her superior army and navy, could easily defeat the rebels.

- However, neither side had universal support. Two-thirds of the population of the colonies either supported the British or did not care either way. Many in Britain did not like the idea of fighting people they regarded as fellow Britons, and were concerned that the war would be expensive.

22.3 The early war

1776

- In March 1776, the British left Boston and the Patriots began to invade other colonies in order to provoke further rebellion. Montreal was captured but retaken by the British in May 1776.

- On 4th July 1776, the delegates at the Continental Congress signed their Declaration of Independence. They wanted to show that they were a united group of independent states fighting a war against Britain, rather than a dispersed collection of rebels. They hoped that this would encourage Britain's enemies to join their side.

- The British were reinforced by friendly German troops and, in July 1776, General Howe led an assault on New York. He drove George Washington out of the city and when winter came, not expecting further fighting, he stood down his troops until the warmer spring weather.

- Washington's men began an assault on Christmas Day, defeating British and allied troops at Trenton and Princeton in New Jersey.

1777

- The British General Burgoyne proposed to cut off the New England colonies from the rest by marching his army south along the Hudson River. In doing so he managed to capture Ticonderoga, Hubbardton and Fort Edward.

- Meanwhile, General Howe attacked Philadelphia, the apparent capital of the colonies, by sea, and successfully captured the city.

- Seven thousand colonials, under the command of General Gates, built entrenchments at Bemis Heights, Saratoga, in order to stop the British march southward. Gates was aided by two notable colonels, Daniel Morgan and Benedict Arnold.

- The British arrived on 19th September and mounted a three-pronged attack. As they advanced through the dense forests, Colonel Morgan's riflemen ambushed them from the trees. Morgan was supported by reinforcements from Colonel Arnold.

- General Burgoyne's troops were themselves reinforced and managed to drive the colonials away, but suffered the loss of 600 men. The British supply line was cut and the troops became desperate for food, while local militias joined the colonials.

- On 7th October, British and German troops left their entrenchments to gather food. They were attacked and driven back by General Arnold's militia, who attempted to break the British line. They nearly succeeded, but Arnold was wounded and, without his leadership, the attack faltered.

- General Burgoyne managed to hold his position but had lost a further 600 men. He finally surrendered on 17th October, and the British moved north into Canada, virtually abandoning their control over the 13 colonies.

- The Patriot victories encouraged the French to join in and support them against Britain; Spain and the Netherlands soon followed. British colonies were now threatened all over the world.

The Battle of Bemis Heights

22.4 The later war

1778–1783

- The British changed tack and decided to encourage loyal supporters to rise up against the rebels. They believed that there were plenty of Loyalists still living in the southern colonies.

- This new campaign began well, led by General Lord Cornwallis, with the British regaining control over Georgia, and South and North Carolina. However, there were not as many southern Loyalists as they had hoped and, once the British moved out of an area, their few supporters were open to attack.

- In 1781, Cornwallis defeated General Nathanael Greene at the Battle of Guilford Courthouse, but began to run out of supplies. He decided to try and meet another British force led by Benedict Arnold, who had since changed sides, in Virginia. The two forces set up their base at Yorktown, which stood on a small peninsula in Chesapeake Bay.

- Meanwhile, George Washington had heard that a French fleet was operating in Chesapeake Bay. He marched part of his army south into Virginia, leaving enough behind to fool General Clinton into thinking that he intended to attack the British in New York.

- The French fleet in Chesapeake Bay forced the British ships away and prevented them from unloading supplies to their troops in Yorktown. In the meantime, Washington's forces approached them by land and trapped them on the peninsula. The British surrendered on 19th October.

- The American War of Independence was now effectively over. A new British government, opposed to the war, began to bring the troops back home, and Britain began to concentrate on maintaining control over its other colonies. The British defeated threats from the French in India and the West Indies, and from the French and Spanish in Gibraltar.

- The Peace of Paris, signed in 1783, formally ended the fighting in America.

Sample question

Try this sample essay question for yourself. A suggested answer is given at the back of the book.

Q. (a) Describe the events of the later American War of Independence between 1778 and 1883. (20)

(b) Explain why these events led to a British defeat. (10)

✓ Draw a chart with several branches to help you remember the events of the American War of Independence. On one branch, record the key battles such as Bunker Hill and Saratoga. Draw other branches to outline the events that led to the war breaking out, the names of the most important generals involved and the countries who joined the war on both sides.

Summary

You should now know the following:

1.   The events surrounding the Stamp Tax, Boston Massacre and Boston Tea Party.

2.   The immediate events that led to the outbreak of war.

3.   The course of the early war of 1776–77.

4.   The course of the later war, leading to peace.

Test yourself

Before moving on to the next chapter, make sure you can answer the following questions. The answers are at the back of the book.

1.   Which restrictive Acts did the British government pass in response to the Boston Tea Party?

2.   Who commanded the British during the battles of Lexington and Concord?

3.   Which two colonels assisted General Gates at Bemis Heights?

4.   At which battle in Virginia did General Cornwallis defeat General Greene in 1781?

Chapter 23: The French Revolution and the Napoleonic Wars

23.1 The French Revolution

France was Britain's main colonial rival, and wanted to expand and maintain its empire, but there was widespread discontent among the French people.

- France was bankrupt after supporting the Patriots in the American War of Independence.

- The poor and the middle classes had to pay taxes while the nobility, which controlled the military and the Church, did not have to.

- People did not receive fair trials or have access to the law. The system was run by the aristocracy, who had been chosen not because of their ability, but by who their ancestors were.

- Prices were rising due to poor harvests and people were starving, unable to grow or buy produce.

Course of the revolution

- Parliament (the Estates General) met in 1789 and discussed these problems. They concluded that the monarchy and aristocracy were at the root of a corrupt system.

- Riots broke out in Paris and the Bastille, a royal fortress, was taken over by the mob. They forced the nobles and clergy out of Parliament, which now renamed itself the National Assembly.

- Tribunals were set up against those who were suspected of being connected with the old regime. King Louis XVI and Queen Marie Antoinette were executed in 1793.

- Other European countries supported the aims of the revolution but were horrified by the violence in France. Leaders worried that the idea would spread to their countries.

- To stop the spread of revolution, France was invaded by Prussia and Austria. The French raised huge armies which defeated the invaders.

- In 1799 the army took over the Assembly, disbanded it and set up General Napoleon Bonaparte as Emperor of France. He wiped out the old corruption and supported fair principles but effectively ruled as a king.

23.2 William Pitt the Younger

- William Pitt, the son of Pitt the Elder (see page 123), became Prime Minister aged just 24 and served for 17 years.

- He improved Britain's economy after the American War of Independence by reforming the tax system, clamping down on smuggling, and removing corrupt government officials.

- The British were particularly worried that revolutionary ideas would spread from France, and radicals in Britain were already supporting this. The government instead gave support to the loyalists, who opposed the radicals.

- Pitt suspended the right of *habeas corpus* – the rule that people cannot be arrested and held indefinitely without a trial. The government also outlawed large public meetings and trade unions.

- Pitt also persuaded other countries to fight by promising money and arms if they declared war on France.

- His military tactic was to use the British navy to blockade the French in their own ports, and to seize the French colonies so that Britain could grow wealthier from an expanded empire.

- The French ignored the British navy and, knowing that they had a large army, instead provoked countries such as Spain, Prussia and Austria into a land war.

23.3 Horatio Nelson

- Nelson proved himself an able military commander at battles such as St Vincent in 1797, where he showed remarkable bravery. He had confidence in the navy, and in battle sought to fight as aggressively as possible.

- He inspired loyalty among his crew and shared his plans willingly with them, trusting them to act appropriately in battle. This was a technique that became known as 'the Nelson Touch'.

- Nelson became notorious for his affair with the wife of the British ambassador in Naples, Lady Emma Hamilton, who was attracted by his heroism. Despite being already married, he had a daughter, Horatia, by her.

- In 1798, Nelson sought to destroy the French fleet that accompanied Napoleon Bonaparte in the Mediterranean. He drew them into an overnight battle at Aboukir Bay in Egypt, and destroyed 11 of France's 13 most important ships.

- In 1800, Sweden, Norway, Denmark, Russia and Prussia formed an alliance against the British. Nelson drew the Danish fleet into battle the following year, although he was under the command of Admiral Sir Hyde Parker. When Parker signalled to retreat, Nelson supposedly placed his telescope on his blind eye and said 'I really do not see the signal'. His tactics paid off and Denmark surrendered.

23.4 The Trafalgar campaign

Napoleon Bonaparte formed an alliance with Spain and planned to invade Britain with them in 1805. Nelson was tasked to prevent this huge navy from reaching the English Channel.

Map showing the location of the Battle of Trafalgar

- At first, the French Admiral Villeneuve managed to evade Nelson and reached Cadiz, on the Spanish coast. Nelson returned to Britain, set out again, and the two fleets met off Cape Trafalgar on 21st October.

- Nelson's tactic was to use two columns of British ships to break through the enemy lines and engage and defeat small portions of their fleet, one at a time. One column was led by his ship, HMS *Victory*, the other by Admiral Collingwood's, HMS *Royal Sovereign*.

- The *Royal Sovereign* reached the enemy first and broke their lines. The Spanish and French gunners were inexperienced and the bad weather made it difficult to fire accurately.

- The *Victory* engaged the French warship the *Redoubtable*, which returned with musket fire. Nelson was hit by a musket ball and died a few hours later as the enemy were surrendering – his last words were 'Thank God, I have done my duty'.

- Nelson's death caused widespread mourning all over Britain. He had managed to destroy the French threat and now British ships had dominance once again over the seas. However, Napoleon still held most of Europe.

23.5 Arthur Wellesley, Duke of Wellington

- Arthur Wellesley, the son of a minor noble, proved himself an excellent military administrator and tactician during campaigns in India.

- Napoleon tried to stop all European countries from trading with Britain and, when Portugal and Spain refused, he invaded both countries. This sparked the Peninsular War as Britain sent a force to defeat the French there.

- Wellesley achieved decisive victories in Portugal in 1808 and 1809, and during the following years kept up the pressure on the French.

The peninsula of Spain and Portugal, location of the Peninsular War

- In 1812, he led an advance into Spain and the following year won the Battle of Vitoria, decisively forcing the French out of the country.

- As the British advanced into France, and faced with the Russians, Austrians and Prussians on another front, Napoleon surrendered and was sent into exile on the island of Elba.

- Wellesley was given the title of Duke of Wellington in recognition of his achievements.

- Napoleon escaped from exile in 1815 and regained power in France. As the allies again declared war, he moved the French army northwards to what is now Belgium. The two armies there were the Prussians, led by Marshal Blücher, and an Anglo-Dutch army, led by Wellington.

23.6 The Waterloo campaign

- Napoleon forced the Anglo-Dutch and Prussian armies to retreat during some skirmishes before the Battle of Waterloo. On the evening of 17th June 1815, Wellington lined his army up on the Mont St Jean ridge, blocking the road to Brussels. He hoped that he could hold out against the French for long enough to be reinforced by Blücher's army.

- The French army opened fire at 1pm the following day. Napoleon intended to break the Anglo-Dutch line and force them away from the advancing Prussians. His initial advance was thrown back by the British cavalry, who nonetheless suffered heavy losses.

- Wellington reorganised his troops on the ridge but this was mistaken for a retreat. The French Marshal Ney sent his cavalry to attack the centre of the British line at 4pm. But instead of retreating in disarray, the British remained in well-disciplined squares.

- By 6pm the French had nearly broken the Anglo-Dutch line. Napoleon could have ordered his elite units, the Imperial Guard, to attack, but he was distracted by the Prussian advances on his right. The French cavalry was unable to advance further without infantry support.

- The Imperial Guard was finally sent in one hour later. As they charged up the ridge, British soldiers who had been lying on the ground got up and fired at point-blank range. As the French retreated, Wellington ordered the whole of his army to advance.

A map of the battlefield of Waterloo on the morning of 18th June 1815

- Napoleon fled the battlefield, but surrendered to the British and, this time, was sent into exile in St Helena in the South Atlantic, where he died in 1821.

✓ Creating a set of index cards might help you remember key facts about the French Revolution and the Napoleonic Wars. Create one or two index cards for each sub-topic: the course of the revolution, William Pitt's foreign policy, Trafalgar and Waterloo. On one side of each card, write out all the big questions you might need to answer; on the other side write the answers to the questions.

You might also want to create index cards about Horatio Nelson and Arthur Wellesley.

Evidence question

You may be asked to answer an evidence question on the Battles of Trafalgar and Waterloo. Refer to the guidance on pages xi–xii and make sure that you practise answering these questions.

Summary

You should now know the following:

1. The key causes and events of the French Revolution.

2. The key events in the lives and careers of William Pitt the Younger, Horatio Nelson and Arthur Wellesley.

3. The key events of the Trafalgar campaign.

4. The key events of the Waterloo campaign.

Test yourself

Before moving on to the next chapter, make sure you can answer the following questions. The answers are at the back of the book.

1. Which new name did the French Parliament give itself after 1789?

2. What is the name of the rule of law which holds that people cannot be arrested and held indefinitely without a trial?

3. At which Mediterranean battle in 1798 did Nelson destroy most of the French ships?

4. Nelson was hit and killed by a musket ball fired from which French ship?

5. At which battle in 1812 did Arthur Wellesley force the French out of Spain?

6. Where was Napoleon Bonaparte exiled to in 1814?

Chapter 24: Dissent and calls for political reform, 1815–1848

24.1 The rise of protest

- The Napoleonic wars had provided work for the textile, iron and coal industries, but once peace was declared, factories closed and jobs were lost. The industrial towns in the Midlands and north of England were hit hardest.

- The government needed to recoup the money it had spent on the war and so placed taxes on goods such as tea, tobacco, sugar and beer.

- Now that cheap corn could be imported from abroad, British farmers were worried that these prices would undercut theirs. This was addressed by the Corn Laws of 1815, which placed a tax on foreign imports of corn.

- Advances in technology meant that people became unemployed because they were replaced by far more efficient machines.

- The rise in prices and lack of jobs caused protests to spring up, particularly in the industrial towns where the people suffered most. Those in fear of being replaced by technology began to smash the new machines. They became known as 'Luddites'.

- Because only wealthy men could vote, it was felt that Parliament was not sympathetic to the poor, and that reform was needed to allow the election of members who understood them. A large protest meeting was held in St Peter's Fields, Manchester, on 16th August 1819, to demand reform in Parliament. A group of local cavalry militia were told to keep order but charged the crowds with their swords drawn. Around a dozen people were killed, and many injured, and the incident was dubbed 'Peterloo' by the press.

- Lord Liverpool, the Prime Minister, felt it essential to deal with the radicals before they became too violent, and the government passed the restrictive Six Acts in 1819. These banned public meetings, gave more powers to magistrates in dealing with protesters and suspended the rule of *habeas corpus* (see page 133).

- In 1820, the Cato Street Conspiracy was uncovered – a plot to assassinate key politicians, overthrow the government and establish revolutionary rule. The plotters were executed and the affair seemed to confirm the government's concerns.

> ✓ Can you draw a map of all the reasons why people protested in Britain in the period from 1815 to 1848? Start with a title in the centre such as 'Reasons for protest' and create a branch coming out of the centre for each distinctive reason you can identify (for example: technological advances). Add short notes and pictures on the branches to remind you of how each reason came about and why it drove people to violent and non-violent forms of resistance.

24.2 The Reform Acts

- Before 1832 every English county, regardless of size, could elect two MPs, whereas Welsh and Scottish counties could only elect one. Men had to own at least 40 shillings' worth of land in order to vote, so fewer than one in 12 men could do so.

- The vast majority of MPs came from towns, and were elected according to outdated and unfair rules dating back over 400 years. Some 'rotten boroughs', containing fewer than 40 voters, still sent two MPs to Parliament.

- There was no secret ballot and voting was done openly. Voters could be bribed to vote for a particular person, or threatened if they did not vote the way others wanted them to.

The Reform Bills in Parliament

- Many believed that reform was necessary, but wanted to introduce it gradually. The new Whig government, led by Earl Grey, put forward a Reform Bill for Parliament to debate in 1831, but it was opposed by a majority.

- Earl Grey had the support of an activist, Thomas Attwood, who formed the Birmingham Political Union, to press for change. He was not trusted by other radicals who felt that he was too open to debate and not enough to action, but the BPU was popular with the working classes.

- A second Reform Bill was introduced in 1832. In the meantime, the Whigs had won a sizeable majority in Parliament and the Bill was passed, only to be thrown out by the Tory majority in the House of Lords. Several riots broke out at this news.

- Grey asked King William IV to create more Whig Lords in order to get the Bill passed. The King refused and Grey resigned as Prime Minister, only to return when the Duke of Wellington was unable to form an alternative government.

- The King was now willing to create new Lords, but such was the pro-reform feeling that this was now unnecessary. The third Bill, known as the Great Reform Bill, was passed with a massive majority on 7th June 1832.

Consequences of the 1832 Great Reform Bill

- Out of a population of 24 million people, the electorate probably increased from 500,000 to 813,000.

- One out of every seven men could now vote. The worst 'rotten boroughs' were abolished and their electorate taken up by larger towns.

- Voters were still wealthy men and there was still no secret ballot.

- MPs were unpaid and so needed plenty of private money and spare time to serve in Parliament. So it took some time for middle-class MPs to be elected, although middle-class politicians became more active in local government.

- The political party system began to take shape in order to attract new voters. The popular support meant that Parliament no longer needed as much royal approval, and so the Crown's control over the political system began to decrease.

- In the village of Tolpuddle, Dorset, a group of six men founded a society to protest against the low wages given to agricultural workers. They were arrested in 1834 and transported to Australia, but a huge public outcry forced their pardon and return.

Evidence question

You may be asked to answer an evidence question on the Great Reform Bill of 1832. Refer to the guidance on pages xi–xii and make sure that you practise answering these questions.

24.3 Chartism

The staunchest radicals believed that the Reform Bill did not go far enough. They also felt that the Acts passed supposedly for their benefit were in fact a way of the government controlling them: by establishing police forces, or by restricting the hours people could work in mines.

Chartism's Six Points

The Chartists wanted Parliament to adopt their Six Points:

- Universal manhood suffrage – the right to vote for all men over the age of 21.

- Secret ballot – so that nobody could be pressured to vote against their wishes.

- Annual parliaments, rather than every seven years – so that Parliament would be more accountable to the voters.

- Abolition of property qualifications for MPs – so that men did not have to be wealthy to be elected.

- Salaries for MPs – so that men did not need private incomes or spare time in order to serve in Parliament.

- Equal electoral districts – so that each MP represented the same number of voters.

A petition to adopt the Six Points gained 1.2 million signatures in 1839.

The petitions of Chartism

- The Chartism movement never had one leader, and different men led certain aspects at different times.

- William Lovett published the Six Points. He wished all men to be educated, and supported peaceful protest – the moral force.

- Fergus O'Connor was an Irish MP and lawyer. He supported violent protest – the physical force – if peaceful protest had failed.

- The Chartists presented their petition to Parliament in May 1839, but it was clear that Parliament had no intention of applying it. The middle classes, who disliked the idea of physical force, began to leave the movement.

- A riot broke out in Newport, South Wales, when an attempt was made to free Chartists held in prison there. The authorities used armed soldiers to control the mob and around 20 rioters were killed. Parliament used the violence as an excuse to arrest key Chartist leaders.

- The Chartists raised a second petition in 1842 and gained two million signatures.

- In the Midlands and north of England a series of protests known as the Plug Riots took place, where workers pulled the plugs from their steam engines, bringing industrial production to a halt. These were probably not Chartist actions but the leaders were still arrested.

- The Chartists raised a third petition in 1848 and, on 10th April, attempted to march on London to present it to Parliament. The government evacuated Queen Victoria and raised an army to stop the 20,000 marchers from reaching Westminster.

- Eventually O'Connor and a few others delivered the petition personally, but when it was discovered that half of the six million signatures had been faked, Parliament refused to discuss it.

Chartism reviewed

- Chartism lacked a strong single leader and was unable to hold on to many of its supporters who did not like the idea of violent protest.

- Both Whig and Tory governments were opposed to the idea of further reform after 1832 and neither wanted to discuss the Chartist petitions.

- However, it is interesting today to see how many of the Six Points were eventually applied to the UK's Parliamentary system.

Evidence question

You may be asked to answer an evidence question on Chartism. Refer to the guidance on pages xi–xii and make sure that you practise answering these questions.

Summary

You should now know the following:

1.   The reasons for the increase in protests during the early 19th century.

2.   The provisions of the Reform Act and its progress through Parliament.

3.   The aims of the Chartists and course of their protests.

Test yourself

Before moving on to the next chapter, make sure you can answer the following questions. The answers are at the back of the book.

1.   Where was the 1820 conspiracy against the British government discovered?

2.   Which name was given to constituencies with a very small number of voters?

3.   Who attempted to form a government on the resignation of Earl Grey in 1832?

4.   Which leader of Chartism published the Six Points and supported the moral force?

Chapter 25: The Agricultural and Industrial Revolutions

25.1 The Agricultural Revolution

Background

- In the early part of the 18th century most British farming worked on the 'open field' system. The land surrounding a village was jointly owned by all the farmers, who all farmed the same crop on each shared field. The crops were grown in rotation, and every three years a field was left fallow, or unseeded, in order for the soil to recover its nutrients.

- On land unsuitable for crops, livestock would be reared. They could also graze on common ground where wood could also be gathered for fires. These animals would be slaughtered in the autumn and the meat stored over winter.

- Word began to spread about new methods of farming that produced higher yields and a better quality of produce.

New methods

- A new type of crop-rotation system, where crops such as turnips or clover were sown during the fallow year, was introduced in the 1730s. The livestock could eat this produce and be kept alive over the winter.

- In the 1760s, Robert Bakewell experimented with the selective breeding of cattle and sheep. He only allowed males and females with good characteristics to mate. This produced sheep with both good quality meat and good quality fleeces, and cows that did not have to be fed as much. Bakewell's animals were hired out to other farmers for breeding with their own stock.

- A writer named Arthur Young produced a book of new ideas, *A Course of Experimental Agriculture*, that became popular among farmers. Young gained a government post and advised farmers on the best agricultural practices.

New technology

- In 1701, Jethro Tull invented the seed drill, which planted the corn in neat rows. Then the Rotherham plough, which could be operated by one man and fewer horses, appeared in 1730.

- Other new inventions to make farmers' lives easier included the iron ploughshare, the reaping machine and the threshing gin.

- Farmers were keen to use the new techniques, but they would only work if a farmer used the same crops every year. The old system of land use would not allow it, so increasingly land became 'enclosed' – that is, a farmer had his portion of land fenced off and permanently allocated to him. This was a complicated procedure and it did not work for all farmers, especially those who were suspicious of the new methods.

142

Jethro Tull's seed drill, 1701

- Farming families began to move out of the villages and into farmhouses adjoining their own enclosed land. Those who did not prosper under the new system gave up farming, and moved away to the towns and cities, taking up industrial jobs.

25.2 The Industrial Revolution

New technology and ideas also brought new techniques to Britain's traditional industries. This Industrial Revolution was to transform the working practices of the country and increase Britain's wealth substantially.

Iron

- Traditionally, iron was made by smelting – the process of heating iron ore and limestone together by burning charcoal. This produced pig iron, which was easy to work with, but not very strong. It could be melted into moulds to form cast iron, which was stronger but could be brittle.

- The trouble with this process was that charcoal was difficult and expensive to produce. Coal was an alternative, but it contained sulphur, which weakened the iron.

- In 1707, Abraham Darby discovered that the sulphur could be removed from coal by burning it in a confined space to produce 'coke'. As a cheaper and more plentiful alternative to charcoal, coke was very successful.

- Darby established an ironworks in Coalbrookdale in Shropshire, where, despite being a pacifist, he produced iron weapons and ammunition for the war against France.

- Darby's son, Abraham Darby II, heard of a primitive steam engine in nearby Dudley that could be used to work the bellows in the furnaces – a system much more efficient than their existing pumps, which were powered by a waterwheel.

- Cast iron was strong, but too brittle to be worked by hand. In 1784, Henry Cort patented a method of producing wrought iron from pig iron by 'puddling' – heating the iron with coal in a separate chamber, to prevent contamination with sulphur. This method took off and wrought iron became more popular than cast iron because it was far easier to work with.

Textiles

- By the 18th century cloth was replacing wool as Britain's most popular textile. The process of making cloth from cotton was long and complicated, but the increased demand caused new ideas and technologies to be developed.

- In 1733, John Kay invented a weaving loom with a 'flying shuttle' that was mechanised and sped up the weaving process. This caused textile workers to fear for their jobs and Kay was attacked several times. Now that thread could be woven so quickly, the thread itself could not be produced quickly enough to satisfy demand.

- James Hargreaves invented the spinning jenny in 1764, which was expanded upon by Richard Arkwright five years later. It consisted of a long line of individual spindles that could all be worked by one waterwheel, producing large amounts of cotton thread in a small amount of time.

- Arkwright set up his machine in Cromford in Derbyshire, where he provided homes, a school, a chapel and an inn for his workers. In return, their wages were cheap and Arkwright was able to operate his mill 24 hours a day, using a shift system.

- Workers now had a set time for starting and finishing work, and rules that governed what they were asked to do – although these were set by their own employer.

Evidence question

You may be asked to answer an evidence question on the cotton industry. Refer to the guidance on pages xi–xii and make sure that you practise answering these questions.

Steam power

- These new industries needed a lot of power to run. Water was one solution, but this was not always reliable. Abraham Darby II had installed a steam engine in his coalworks (see above) and this encouraged other industries to do the same.

- In 1712, Thomas Newcomen invented an 'atmospheric steam engine' to pump water out of mines. This was very effective and popular, but was huge and difficult to transport, and had to be constructed on site by either Newcomen or inexperienced workers trying to follow instructions.

- James Watt felt he could improve on this, and worked on the idea of a 'perfect steam engine'. Watt had the scientific ideas but not the industrial setup to manufacture the working engines. In 1773, he became business partners with an industrialist, Matthew Boulton, and the two men went into production. Within 25 years they had built more than 500 working steam engines, and won many legal cases against those who attempted to steal their ideas and methods.

- Boulton and Watt became rich from their invention but their engines only accounted for about 30 per cent of all steam engines made in Britain during the 18th century. Improved Newcomen engines were still popular and in some cases were regarded as more reliable.

✓ Draw a flow chart with a branch for each area in which new technologies and methods changed the way people worked in the early 18th century: agriculture, iron working, textiles and steam power. Try to capture the key information about each new technology or method. Make sure you do not muddle the order in which things were invented. Consider drawing small diagrams, cartoons or other visual cues to remind you of the details, e.g. a pig to represent pig iron.

Summary

You should now know the following:

1. The old methods and techniques that were superseded by the Industrial and Agricultural Revolutions.

2. The new methods and techniques that were introduced during the Industrial and Agricultural Revolutions.

3. Key developments in the history of the iron and textile industries.

4. The importance of steam power to the Industrial Revolution.

Test yourself

Before moving on to the next chapter, make sure you can answer the following questions. The answers are at the back of the book.

1. Which farmer experimented with selective breeding in the 1760s?

2. What is the name of the process by which wrought iron is produced from pig iron?

3. Who invented the flying shuttle in 1733?

4. Which industrialist went into business with the inventor James Watt?

Chapter 26: The transportation revolution

The Agricultural and Industrial Revolutions meant that goods and people needed to be transported around the country more efficiently than they had been before. Transport by ship could only go so far, and many roads inland were not being maintained by the local councils.

26.1 Roads

- From the late 17th century, Parliament gave local landowners the right to set up turnpike trusts. These would be responsible for the upkeep of a section of road and in return could charge a toll to those who travelled along it.

- The trusts employed specialist builders to maintain the road surfaces. John McAdam devised a method of laying a road with medium-sized stones, then laying small chips of granite on top. The weight of the carts passing over them compressed the chippings into a 'macadam' surface. Later on, when tar was added, this became known as 'tarmacadam' and then 'tarmac'.

- Stagecoaches took advantage of these improved roads. They travelled in stages, typically stopping at inns to change horses, and carried post and newspapers as well as people.

- As the coach services improved with the roads, journey times fell. In 1658 the journey from London to Exeter took 96 hours – 200 years later it took only one-sixth of that time.

- Some objected to the tolls, especially in times of agricultural depression. In South Wales between 1839 and 1844, men disguised as women attacked the tollgates. These incidents became known as the 'Rebecca Riots'.

26.2 Canals

- Canals, or man-made rivers, offered the opportunity of sailing to places that rivers did not reach. In 1758 Francis Egerton, the third Duke of Bridgewater, had the idea of building a canal between his coal mines in Worsley and the city of Manchester.

- Egerton commissioned James Brindley as his chief engineer for the project, and Brindley produced a canal that included such remarkable feats as the Barton aqueduct over the River Irwell. Brindley was then employed to build several more canals by other industrialists.

- To build a canal, an Act of Parliament was required to force landowners to sell their land to the project. Then a workforce was needed to transport the materials to the site and to dig out the foundations. These men were known as navigators, shortened to 'navvies'.

- Canals were extremely expensive to build and took a long time to complete. But they became an extremely popular transport option and their owners could profit greatly from the toll charges on them.

- The war against France in the late 18th century diverted funds away from canals and they stopped being built. But the building resumed in the early 19th century and by 1840 Britain had 4,000 miles of navigable canals open for use.

These two maps show how many canals were built in Britain between 1760 and 1820

26.3 Rail

- The railways came about thanks to developments in both steam power and the production of iron (see page 143).

- A Cornish engineer named Richard Trevithick experimented with the power of steam under pressure. In 1804 he produced a locomotive that was capable of pulling wagons between Merthyr Tydfil and the Glamorganshire Canal in South Wales. Four years later he built the *Catch-Me-Who-Can*, a locomotive on a circular track giving rides at 19km per hour. Trevithick died penniless but his ideas were used by others.

- George Stephenson was appointed chief engineer of the Stockton and Darlington goods railway, which opened in 1825 and ran for 27 miles. He was then appointed chief engineer for the planned Liverpool to Manchester railway, and overcame many challenges to successfully build it.

- The authorities still needed convincing that steam was the most appropriate method to power the locomotives. A series of trials, to determine the most efficient engine, was held at Rainhill, near Liverpool, in October 1829. Stephenson's *Rocket* was the outright winner, achieving a speed of 48km per hour.

- The Liverpool and Manchester railway opened in September 1830 and was a great success, despite the accidental death of William Huskisson, an MP who was hit by the *Rocket* on the opening day. Unlike the Stockton and Darlington railway, its main purpose was to carry passengers, and its success began a boom in the number of railways being built in Britain. By 1852, over 6,000 miles of railway track had been laid.

- The stagecoach and canal operators lost out from the coming of the railways. But they boosted important industries and helped to extend the Industrial Revolution. They also helped people to travel, both for work and for holidays – it was no longer necessary to live within walking distance of your job, or to stay at home during your free time.

You could map out the different ways in which transport was revolutionised in Britain. Start with a central bubble labelled 'the transportation revolution' and create separate branches for roads, canals and railways, recording the key facts about how each form of transport was developed.

Sample question

Try this sample essay question for yourself. A suggested answer is given at the back of the book.

Q.   (a) Describe the key developments in the coming of the railways.   (20)

      (b) Explain why the railways were so important to the country as a whole.   (10)

26.4 Telford and Brunel

Thomas Telford (1757–1834)

- Thomas Telford trained as a stonemason but had no formal training in architecture or engineering. As surveyor for public works in Shropshire he was asked to become involved in building the Ellesmere Canal in 1793.

- Telford was also involved in road building but, through building many challenging bridges and aqueducts, proved that he was most proficient working with iron. Among his notable achievements were the Pontcysyllte Aqueduct and the London to Holyhead road, which included the magnificent Menai Suspension Bridge.

Isambard Kingdom Brunel (1806–1859)

- Isambard Kingdom Brunel was the son of the engineer Marc Brunel. His design for the Clifton Suspension Bridge in Bristol was rejected by Thomas Telford but went on to be selected as the final design.

- Brunel had been on the Liverpool and Manchester railway, and wanted to make rail travel smoother and more efficient. In 1833 he planned the route of the Great Western Railway between Bristol and London, and supervised its construction over the next nine years.

- As well as railways, Brunel worked on the Great Exhibition in 1851, a design for a prefabricated hospital in 1855 and various ocean liners – all with varying success.

✓ You might benefit from filling in a table like the one below, listing the engineers, inventors and builders who contributed to the revolution in transportation. Write down what they achieved in their lifetimes and also, if you can, the impact their work had.

Name of person	Achievements	Impact
John McAdam	Invented the 'macadam' road surface	Stagecoaches took advantage of the new roads and journey times fell.

Summary

You should now know the following:

1.   The changes to Britain's network of roads during the transportation revolution.

2.   The introduction of canals to Britain during the transportation revolution.

3.   The invention and introduction of railways to Britain during the transportation revolution.

4.   Key events in the lives of Thomas Telford and Isambard Kingdom Brunel, and their roles in the transportation revolution.

Test yourself

Before moving on to the next chapter, make sure you can answer the following questions. The answers are at the back of the book.

1.   Where did the 'Rebecca Riots' take place between 1839 and 1844?

2.   Why did canal building in Britain stop during the late 18th century?

3.   Which passenger railway line, designed by Stephenson, opened in September 1830?

4.   Which suspension bridge in Bristol was designed by Brunel?

Chapter 27: Social and industrial reform

27.1 The slave trade

- Slavery had been part of British life for several hundred years, although many ordinary people never used slaves.

- By the system known as the 'triangular trade', ships carried goods made in Britain, such as cloth, to Africa where they were traded for slaves. The ships then sailed to the Americas, where the slaves were sold in return for raw materials such as sugar or cotton, which were taken back to Britain for manufacturing.

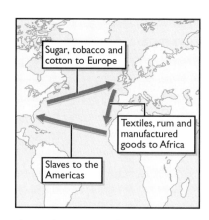

A modern map showing the triangular trade

- Sometimes the slaves bought in Africa were ordinary citizens who had been kidnapped to be sold. They were forced on to ships that had been designed to carry as many people as possible.

- In the case of the slave ship *Zong*, the captain found that most of his cargo were ill or dying. Because he could claim their value from his insurers if they died at sea, many of the sick slaves were thrown overboard to drown. As slaves were regarded as property, rather than people, the captain could not be convicted of murder.

- Most slaves on British ships went to the West Indies, where they were put to work in sugar plantations while they were still children.

- Slaves in the West Indies were subjected to brutal punishments and this, together with the poor conditions and diet, meant that they lived only short lives.

Evidence question

You may be asked to answer an evidence question on the slave trade. Refer to the guidance on pages xi–xii and make sure that you practise answering these questions.

27.2 The abolition movement

- The Quakers, a group of pacifist Christians, were the first people to stand up against slavery in Britain.

- A non-Quaker named Granville Sharp met a young black slave in London, named Jonathan Strong, who had been physically abused by his owner. Sharp and his brother cared for Strong until his owner spotted him and attempted to sell him on. Sharp took his case to law and Strong was released.

- Sharp and the Quakers then became involved in other legal cases relating to slavery. A group of them formed the Society for the Abolition of the Slave Trade in 1787, and set out to change people's attitudes toward slavery. Their main spokesman was Thomas Clarkson, who invested a lot of time and money travelling the country and spreading the word.

- The cause was taken up by William Wilberforce, the MP for Hull, who raised questions on the issue in Parliament. Olaudah Equiano, an ex-slave who had written a book on his experiences, toured the country giving readings. Another supporter was the ceramics maker Josiah Wedgwood, who printed anti-slavery designs on his pots.

- The pro-slavery camp argued that losing the slave trade would allow other countries to take over Britain's colonies and achieve greater wealth, and that people had a better life as slaves than they did in Africa. Horatio Nelson declared himself a supporter.

- The anti-slavery campaigners succeeded in getting the Dolben Act passed through Parliament in 1788. This prevented too many slaves from being carried on a ship and forced ships to carry a surgeon to attend to their needs.

- Wilberforce tried but failed to pass anti-slavery Bills through Parliament in 1789 and 1791. The following year, Clarkson produced a book summarising the evidence he had presented to Parliament, which sold well and provoked hundreds of petitions.

- Parliament took steps to introduce laws against slavery, but the war against France intervened in 1793 and they were diverted on to other issues.

The gradual victory

- James Stephen, an anti-slavery lawyer resident in the West Indies, drew up a Bill that Wilberforce put through Parliament in 1806. It banned British ships and sailors from trading slaves with French colonies or allies of France. This seemed reasonable while Britain was fighting the French, and it made the slave trade much less profitable.

- This success encouraged others to take up the cause and the number of anti-slavery MPs in Parliament grew. Finally, in March 1807, a Bill banning the British slave trade passed through Parliament.

- Slavery was not yet completely abolished. New slaves could not be bought, but there were still thousands working on plantations across Britain's colonies. Their owners started to treat them better so that they were able to work for longer.

- The campaigners called for immediate abolition. They publicised the story of a young white missionary named John Smith, who had died in prison after encouraging a group of slaves in Guyana to revolt against their owners.

The final victory

- The Great Reform Act of 1832 meant that many anti-slavery MPs lost their seats in Parliament, and the cause was weakened.

- Meanwhile, the slaves in the West Indies had heard about the steps being taken in Britain and they were getting restless. As more revolts broke out the government became concerned about a full-scale rebellion against British rule.

- A compromise was reached in Parliament in 1833. It was suggested that only slave children under six years old would be freed immediately – the rest would have to work as apprentices for their masters before being freed. The owners would also be compensated for losing their slaves.

- The Emancipation Act was passed in 1834, but the anti-slavery campaigners were angered by the compromises. It took another four years for the whole system to be dismantled and for slavery in Britain's colonies to end completely.

27.3 Prison reform

- As the Industrial Revolution encouraged more people to move into the towns and cities, the urban amenities, including prisons, were overwhelmed. Disease took hold amid the disgusting conditions, and prisoners had no opportunities for their own space or for exercise.

- Elizabeth Fry was a Quaker who visited prisons to attend to the poor. She became increasingly alarmed by the worsening conditions, and gathered a band of helpers who supplied new clothes and clean bedding.

- Fry organised a Ladies' Committee to visit the women prisoners every day. A school for the prisoners' children was started, and the prisoners were encouraged to sew or knit, and to sell their products.

- Her advice was sought by the government for the reform of all prisons. As a Quaker she got rid of 'unhealthy' practices such as gambling, drinking and reading novels, which some resented. Others suggested that she was making prisoners too comfortable and that they were not getting the punishment they deserved.

- The British reforms spread over Europe and soon ladies' committees had been formed in France, and what are now Belgium and Germany.

27.4 Poor Law reform

- In the early 19th century the Poor Laws were over 200 years old. The Poor Rate was paid by villagers to be given to the poor in their own parish, but the rate varied.

- Now the Industrial Revolution had made the old system obsolete, as many had moved into the towns and cities, away from their home parish, and were allowed no relief.

- The Poor Law Commission was set up in 1832. It divided the poor into 'deserving' and 'undeserving' categories, and worked out the terms of the Act that was passed two years later.

The 1834 Poor Act

- Outdoor relief was discouraged. Relief was only offered if the poor were willing to live in a workhouse.

- Parishes were grouped into 'unions' and shared a workhouse between them.

- The rate of relief was standardised across the country.

- The workhouses were deliberately made uncomfortable so that people would be encouraged to leave and seek work themselves.

27.5 Employment reform

- The Industrial Revolution had caused many more of Britain's workforce to be employed by factories. There was very little regard given to the effect that these workplaces had on the health of the employees.

- Children were employed in cotton mills because they were small enough to move under the machinery to sweep up the small pieces of cloth. This was a dangerous environment and the children could easily be killed or maimed by the machines. There were no restrictions on their working hours.

- Some people began to notice the poor conditions, particularly in mines and cotton mills, and began to press for reform. A leading voice was Anthony Ashley Cooper, the seventh Earl of Shaftesbury, who spoke in Parliament on the need for better conditions.

- Some mill owners believed that employees worked better if they were treated well. A Scottish mill owner named Robert Owen regulated the working hours for his workers, and provided education and housing, but not many others followed his example.

- The Ten Hours Movement, set up in 1830, pressed for the working hours of children to be reduced to ten a day. They lost supporters in Parliament after the Great Reform Act of 1832. But Cooper attempted to pass a Bill through Parliament the following year, supported by a commission that had examined conditions in the cotton industry.

- The Bill failed to pass and the government pushed through their own legislation which became the Factory Act.

The Factory Act 1833

- Children under the age of nine were not allowed to work in factories.

- Children under the age of 13 could not work more than nine hours a day.

- Children under the age of 18 could not work more than 12 hours a day.

- Children under the age of 18 were not allowed to work at night.

- All children had to be given two hours of education every day.

Further Factory Acts

- The reformers were very disappointed by the terms of the 1833 Act. The mill owners wanted children to work longer and they were often supported by the child's parents, who needed the extra income. It was also difficult to prove a child's age if the parents were not truthful.

- Parliament did not want to interfere with the relationship between employers and employees. Nonetheless, Cooper continued to press for further reform and succeeded in getting three more Factory Acts passed.

- The Factory Act 1844 banned women from working more than 12 hours a day, and those under 13 from more than six and a half hours.

- The Factory Act 1847 banned both women and children from working more than ten hours.

- The Factory Act 1850 set the daily working hours for women and children as between 6am and 6pm, and required an hour's break for meals.

- In 1888 the women and girls working at the Bryant and May match factory in London went on strike, protesting against the long hours, poor pay and health risks of working with the dangerous phosphorous in the matches. Parliament forced the factory owners to improve conditions.

- London dockworkers went on strike the following year and also succeeded in improving their working conditions.

✓ Use a flow chart with multiple strands to track the progress made by the abolitionists and reformers. The point of the chart is that you do not have to rewrite the whole narrative – just pick out the milestone events and the major figures involved in each struggle, and make use of abbreviations and pictures. For example, on the prison reform strand, start with the horrible conditions in the prisons before reform (disease and lack of space) and continue with Elizabeth Fry's efforts.

Summary

You should now know the following:

1. The facts relating to the slave trade in the late 18th century.

2. The key events that led to the eventual abolition of slavery.

3. The key events surrounding the reform of prisons, led by Elizabeth Fry.

4. The key events surrounding the reform of the Poor Laws.

5. The key events surrounding the reform of employment conditions, led by Anthony Ashley Cooper.

Test yourself

Before moving on to the next chapter, make sure you can answer the following questions. The answers are at the back of the book.

1. Which Quaker was instrumental in first pressing for the abolition of slavery?

2. Which 1788 Act prevented too many slaves from being carried on a ship?

3. What was the name given to the groups founded by Elizabeth Fry that visited women's prisons?

4. Which Act of Parliament set the daily working hours for women and children as between 6am and 6pm?

Chapter 28: A decade of success: the Great Exhibition and the Crimean War

28.1 The Great Exhibition

Britain had achieved much in the years leading up to 1851. Now it wanted to show off these successes to its people and to the world.

- A civil servant named Henry Cole had the idea of the Great Exhibition and set up a competition to design the building that would house it. Eventually the winning design was passed over in favour of one by Joseph Paxton, a garden architect, following his chance meeting with MP John Ellis.

- Paxton's iron and glass building was erected in Hyde Park, taking nine months to build. It was one of the largest buildings in London: 563m long and 139m wide, encompassing a row of elm trees from the park. It became known as the Crystal Palace.

- The Crystal Palace was divided in two: one half for Britain and the Empire; the other for foreign countries. Over 100,000 items went on display from all parts of the world.

- The Great Exhibition opened on 1st May 1851 and admitted 500,000 people. Queen Victoria and Prince Albert officially opened the event.

- Between May and the exhibition's close in October, around four million visitors attended. The admittance charge was £3 but dropped to one shilling on certain days. Group visits were organised by community leaders such as mayors and vicars, and the railways ran special trips to London in order for people to attend.

- The Great Exhibition allowed upper, middle and working classes to mix together and attend the same event. The upper and middle classes were often surprised at how well the working classes behaved. Queen Victoria was even known to attend on 'shilling days' in order to see all classes of her people.

- Prince Albert, who had been one of the chief organisers of the Exhibition, was particularly keen for the profits to be used for cultural foundations. The money was therefore used to found such London attractions as the Royal Albert Hall, and the Victoria and Albert, Science and Natural History Museums.

Sample question

Try this sample essay question for yourself. A suggested answer is given at the back of the book.

Q. (a) Describe the purpose and approach of the Great Exhibition. (20)

(b) Explain its importance and success to the country as a whole. (10)

28.2 The Crimean War

In 1854, Russia marched into the old Ottoman Empire to seize areas of what is now Turkey. Britain and France were concerned that the Russians would dominate the Mediterranean if they conquered land up to Istanbul. They therefore sent troops to the Crimea to attack the Russian port at Sevastopol.

A map showing the Crimean peninsula and the city of Sevastopol

- The British troops were poorly trained and badly equipped. The soldiers suffered sickness and many died before seeing a battle.

- The British supply base at Balaklava was overlooked by Turkish fortifications, which the Russians seized on the morning of 25th October 1854. The British managed to block the Russian advance.

- Then it was decided to send the Light Cavalry Brigade, consisting of 673 men, into a charge against the Russians. They were hopelessly outnumbered and 247 were killed or wounded. The incident was made famous by Tennyson's poem *The Charge of the Light Brigade,* which presented it as an example of British heroism.

- The Russians surrendered Sevastopol and a peace treaty was signed among the nations. The British army had lost 17,000 men in battle and as many again through disease.

- The Crimean War was the first war to be reported by the system of telegraph, a new technology at the time. Journalists covered the war closely and the British public were able to read about events abroad shortly after they occurred.

28.3 Seacole and Nightingale

Mary Seacole (1805–1881)

- Mary Seacole was born in Jamaica to a Scottish officer and a black mother, whose family had originally been slaves. She learnt her medical skills from her mother, who had inherited 'doctoress' skills from the African tradition.

- Mary wanted to go to the Crimea to help the British soldiers she had known in Jamaica, but was initially turned down because she was of mixed race. She eventually arrived in early 1855 and set up the British Hotel near Sevastopol, where she tended to the sick.

- Mary Seacole was noted among the British soldiers for her bravery under fire and her medical skills. After the war she wrote her memoirs and retired quietly in England.

Florence Nightingale (1820–1910)

- Florence Nightingale was born in Florence, Italy, to British parents. She insisted on pursuing nursing as a career despite her parents' objections. She gained some training in Germany and began her nursing career in London.

- Florence was asked to take a party of 38 nurses to the Crimea. At Scutari they found the hospital in an appalling state, and were not welcomed by officers who did not regard theirs as a woman's job.

- Florence's habit was to walk around the wards last thing at night, carrying a small lamp, checking that all was well and asking if patients needed anything. She gained the nickname of the 'Lady with the Lamp'.

- She was also astute with money and managed to raise enough to provide clothing, equipment for the soldiers and even a new, fully working hospital for 80 patients.

- On her return to Britain in 1856, Florence promoted the ideas she had developed and helped to improve ideas about health and social welfare. Despite being in poor health herself, she continued to write and was published in newspapers until her death.

> ✓ Create a set of index cards to help you revise the main events of the 1850s (the Great Exhibition and the Crimean War), and recall the actions of Mary Seacole and Florence Nightingale. On one side of each card list the important questions such as 'Why was the Great Exhibition held?' and 'Why did so many British soldiers die in the Crimean War?'. Record the answers on the flipside.

Summary

You should now know the following:

1.   The purpose and approach of the Great Exhibition.

2.   The key causes and events of the Crimean War.

3.   The achievements of Mary Seacole and Florence Nightingale.

Test yourself

Before moving on to the next chapter, make sure you can answer the following questions. The answers are at the back of the book.

1.   What was the name given to the building housing the Great Exhibition?

2.   On which date was the Battle of Balaklava fought?

3.   What was the name of the hospital set up near Sevastopol by Mary Seacole?

4.   What was the nickname given to Florence Nightingale?

Chapter 29: Queen Victoria, government and politics

29.1 Victoria's life

Queen Victoria, still Britain's longest-serving monarch today, had a reign that spanned a multitude of social, political and cultural changes.

- Victoria was the daughter of Edward, Duke of Kent, and Victoria, Princess of Leiningen. Her father died when she was a child and she fell increasingly under the control of her domineering mother.

- Victoria was the only surviving grandchild of King George III and, as such, was next in line to her uncle, William IV. When William died in June 1837, Victoria became Queen, aged just 18. She immediately moved away from her mother's influence.

- Victoria was known to be beautiful and intelligent, but also headstrong and stubborn. She hated dealing with people she disliked and only wanted to surround herself with friends.

- Victoria married her cousin, Prince Albert of Saxe-Coburg, in 1840. As a foreigner, Albert was viewed with suspicion in Britain but worked hard to gain people's trust. He managed the royal estates and helped to promote cultural attractions for the people.

- When Prince Albert died in 1861 Victoria was devastated and wore mourning clothes for the rest of her life. She shut herself away from the public but still handled affairs of state as efficiently as before.

- Victoria and Albert's children married into other European royal families and strengthened the political ties between Britain and Europe, particularly with Germany and Russia.

- Her Golden and Diamond Jubilees were celebrated in 1887 and 1897 with widespread celebrations throughout the Empire. Victoria died in January 1901, and the throne passed to her eldest son, who became King Edward VII.

29.2 Victorian politics

The Whig Prime Minister Lord Melbourne helped Victoria a great deal with her new position and defended her against those who felt she was unsuitably young. But in 1839 he lost an important debate in Parliament and resigned. The Tory leader Robert Peel was asked to take over but requested that Melbourne's friends in the royal household be replaced with his allies. In what became known as the Bedchamber Crisis, Victoria refused, claiming that her household was her business alone. She was forced to back down when Peel won a general election decisively in 1841.

The repeal of the Corn Laws

- Peel was particularly interested in the economy and promoted 'free trade' – the idea that people should be able to deal in goods across national borders without having to pay import or export taxes.

- Peel was also against changes to the established order, and opposed the 1832 Reform Act and the demands of the Chartists.

- The Corn Laws had been passed in 1815 to protect the price of corn after the Napoleonic wars. Peel argued that they stood against free trade, and that they caused hardship by making the price of bread artificially high. He was not supported by fellow Tories who grew crops on their land.

- The Corn Laws were only repealed because the Whigs supported it; 222 Tories had opposed it and the issue split the party between 'Peelites' and 'Protectionists'.

Gladstone and Disraeli

- William Gladstone and Benjamin Disraeli were on opposite sides of the Tory split. Disraeli opposed Peel, while Gladstone supported him but was not in Parliament at the time.

- Gladstone remained loyal to Peel when his government collapsed, but later joined the Whigs in 1859 and formed a new party, the Liberals.

- Disraeli had a Jewish background and was a successful author before going to Parliament, both of which made him feel like something of an outsider. After the collapse of the Tories he became leader of the Conservative party that was formed to replace them.

- Gladstone led the Liberals to government in 1868 and passed a large number of Acts dealing in social reform. They passed the 1870 Elementary Education Act, which established compulsory free schools for children up to the age of 11. Despite this, Gladstone did not generally feel very strongly about social reform and felt that the poor ought to help themselves.

- In 1886, during his third term in government, Gladstone decided to grant Ireland a small amount of independence, known as Home Rule, in order to control the increasing unrest there. This split the Liberal party and many Liberals joined the Conservatives, who strongly opposed the idea.

- Disraeli also passed reforming acts but valued the Conservative party above everything and would not do anything to provoke a damaging split. Two Factory Acts in 1874 and 1878 reduced working hours, and required working conditions to be inspected and approved by government officials.

- In 1875 Disraeli managed to buy a 44 per cent share in the Suez Canal, which was an important route to Asia, connecting Britain with the Empire. He created the title Empress of India for Queen Victoria and became her favourite politician.

- As the Ottoman Empire declined and Russia declared war on the Turks, Disraeli helped to broker a peace between the nations at the Congress of Berlin in 1878. Britain also gained the island of Cyprus from the Turks.

✓ Try representing the course of Queen Victoria's reign in a flowchart like a pictorial timeline, making sure events are placed in the right order. You could run the dates along one side next to each bubble. Use symbols and pictures to remember the different influences (personal and political) on Victoria.

Sample question

Try this sample essay question for yourself. A suggested answer is given at the back of the book.

Q.   (a) Describe the life and achievements of William Gladstone.   (20)

(b) Explain why his career might be regarded as a failure by some.   (10)

Summary

You should now know the following:

1.   Key events in the life of Queen Victoria.

2.   The major political issues during Victoria's reign.

3.   The roles of William Gladstone and Benjamin Disraeli.

Test yourself

Before moving on to the next chapter, make sure you can answer the following questions. The answers are at the back of the book.

1.   In which year did Prince Albert die?

2.   What was the name given to the crisis caused by Victoria's refusal to change her household staff?

3.   Which 1870 Act established free schooling for children?

4.   Which territory did Britain gain from Turkey in 1878?

Chapter 30: The rise and rise of the British Empire

30.1 India

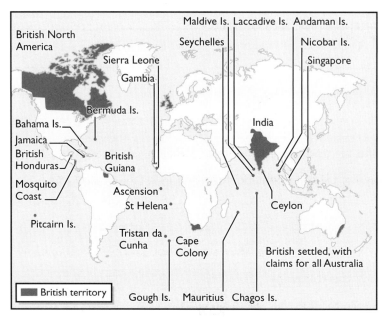

Map of the British Empire at the end of the Napoleonic Wars in 1815

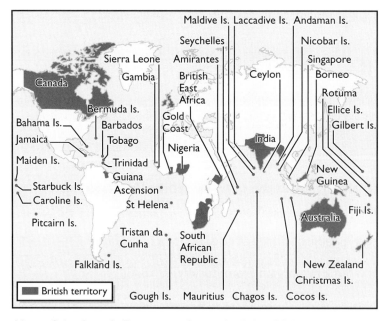

Map of the British Empire at the end of the 19th century

● Britain's interests in India were controlled by the East India Company, founded in 1600, with the trade mainly in goods such as tea, cotton, spices and silk. It worked with local rulers and grew to become the largest trading company in India, seeing off competition from other European powers.

- In 1757, Robert Clive won the Battle of Plassey against the Nawab of Bengal and his French supporters. The East India Company then took over the running of Bengal, collecting taxes and administering the justice systems.

- The East India Company hired local men, known as sepoys, to be trained as soldiers in the British fashion and to give military force to the company's rule.

- As British traders and officers began to settle in Bengal under the company's rule, they brought their wives and families. This caused small pockets of British communities within India, which were distrusted and resented by the local people.

30.2 The Indian Mutiny

- The Indian Mutiny was sparked in Meerut in 1857. The sepoys were given new paper cartridges for their guns which had to be bitten to release the gunpowder. The cartridges had been greased with cow or pig fat which the sepoys, as either Hindus or Muslims, were forbidden to touch. They therefore refused to use them and this, together with discontent about their pay and conditions, caused a mutiny against the British.

- On 29th March, a sepoy named Mangal Pandey shot at a British officer and was executed. His whole regiment was disbanded and the other sepoys lost their jobs.

- On 9th May, 85 sepoys in Meerut were imprisoned for refusing to use their guns. The following day 2,000 others took over the prison and freed them. In the rioting that followed, 50 British men and several women and children were killed.

- The rebels marched to Delhi and proclaimed the Mughal Emperor, Bahadur Shah II, as their leader. Any British person nearby was killed and their weapons seized. As word spread over Bengal, other sepoys mutinied and joined the rebellion.

- The local people also rose up to support the sepoys. Together the rebels surrounded significant British communities, including civilians, at Cawnpore, Lucknow and Delhi.

The Cawnpore massacre

- Three hundred British soldiers and a further 600 civilians were held under siege by rebels under the command of Nana Sahib, a prince who had been forced out of power by the East India Company.

- Sahib promised the British safe conduct out of Cawnpore by boat, but for uncertain reasons the British were attacked as they embarked. All 300 soldiers were killed, along with 400 civilians. The surviving 200 women and children were imprisoned in a house.

- On 15th July, Nana Sahib and his men were defeated by General Henry Havelock. The following day the British discovered that the prisoners had been butchered where they were held, apparently on the orders of Nana Sahib.

- The British were outraged by the massacre and sought their revenge on the sepoys, burning the surrounding villages and killing any sepoy who tried to surrender.

Lucknow

- The 800 British soldiers and 500 civilians in Lucknow were able to shelter in the fortified British Residency there, and initially had access to food and water. But supplies began to run out during August and September.

- General Havelock's troops were reinforced by those of Major-General Sir James Outram, and they were able to advance on Lucknow. They fought their way into the city on 25th September.

- On reaching the British Residency, Havelock and Outram found there were so many sick and wounded that they could not be moved. Instead Havelock joined the beseiged people and sent a message asking for more reinforcements.

- The relief force, under the command of General Colin Campbell, fought its way into Lucknow on 17th November and evacuated the British at the Residency.

- The rebels in Lucknow held out until March 1858, when the city fell back into British hands completely.

Delhi

- As the capital of the Mughal Empire, Delhi was the most significant city to be held under siege. It was important for morale that the British should regain it.

- It took six days for the city to be retaken by the British, which was achieved on 19th September. Bahadur Shah II was captured trying to flee the city.

- The British lost 3,000 men in the battle for Delhi.

- Fighting continued into the following year. Those found guilty of inciting rebellion, or of participating in the massacres, were hanged or blown apart by cannons.

Consequences of the mutiny

- The government looked into the causes of the uprising and found the practices of the East India Company to be at fault.

- The structure of the army was modified to allow locals to achieve higher ranks and British officers were encouraged to mix with the locals.

- The local government in India was also reorganised to allow locals to rise to higher office.

- More respect was paid generally to Indian customs, and traditions that did not conflict with British rule were allowed to continue.

- Nonetheless, Britain was keen to re-establish its rule and discourage any further mutiny. Queen Victoria was given the title Empress of India, which emphasised just who was in charge.

Evidence question

You may be asked to answer an evidence question on the Indian Mutiny. Refer to the guidance on pages xi–xii and make sure that you practise answering these questions.

30.3 South Africa

- South Africa was first taken by the British from the Dutch during the Napoleonic Wars. The Dutch settlers, or Boers, travelled north to establish their own states, the Transvaal and the Orange Free State.

- When diamonds were found on a remote farm in 1871, thousands of people flocked there and established the town of Kimberley. The British annexed the Transvaal in 1877 and defeated the Zulus, who also wanted to regain the land from the Boers.

- Three years later, the Transvaal declared its independence and Britain went to war with the Boers, but eventually agreed peace terms.

- An Englishman, Cecil Rhodes, had controlled the de Beers mining company in Kimberley and now became Governor of Cape Colony. He started mining for gold in the Transvaal and annexed two areas for mining that became known as Northern and Southern Rhodesia.

- The town of Johannesburg was established at the spot where gold was found in the Transvaal. This led to thousands of Uitlanders – or outsiders – coming into the country. Paul Kruger, President of the Transvaal, did not want to give these settlers the vote, which allowed the British to argue that they were being treated unfairly.

- In 1896 Rhodes organised a raid into the Transvaal to provoke the Uitlanders into rebellion. The plot was discovered and Rhodes had to give up his position.

- Sir Alfred Milner, the British High Commissioner, believed that the Boers needed to be pushed out of both the Transvaal and Cape Colony by force. In the meantime, the Boers armed themselves with weapons bought from Germany.

- By October 1899, three groups were ready for war: the British, who had sent 10,000 soldiers to South Africa; the Boers, who had greater experience of fighting in the veld grasslands of South Africa; and the black Africans, who were used as labourers and servants by both sides.

30.4 The Anglo-Boer War, 1899–1902

The Boer War can be divided into three stages:

● The Boer offensives

● The British offensives

● Guerrilla war and stalemate

The Boer offensives

● The Boers acted swiftly and surrounded large British forces at Ladysmith, Mafeking and Kimberley.

● General Sir Redvers Buller sent Lord Methuen to relieve Kimberley and Mafeking, and set out for Ladysmith himself, before planning to march into the Transvaal and Orange Free State.

● The Boers set a trap for Lord Methuen's men at Magersfontein by concealing themselves in hidden trenches and opening fire suddenly – 950 British soldiers were killed.

A map showing where the Boer attacked at the beginning of the war and the early battles of Magersfontein, Colenso and Spion Kop

● Buller's men were also defeated when trying to cross the Tugela River at Colenso. He turned his efforts elsewhere and, together with General Warren, tried to break through the Boer defences surrounding Ladysmith by sending British troops over a hill named Spion Kop.

● The British succeeded in taking the hill on 3rd January 1900, but found themselves surrounded by Boers on neighbouring hills, who bombarded them with artillery fire.

● The British retreated from Spion Kop, but managed to take some nearby high ground named Twin Peaks. The Boers struggled to keep up but inflicted heavy losses on the British – 1,500 men were lost in all.

The British offensives

● Buller was replaced by Lord Roberts, who brought with him an army that was better equipped, with cavalry units. He decided not to attack the Boers head on, but to surround them with British horsemen.

● The new tactic worked at Kimberley, where the siege was lifted on 15th February 1900.

● The Boers, under General Cronje, fled northwards but became trapped at Paardeberg, where they were surrounded by British cavalry. Cronje withstood two weeks of bombardment but surrendered on 27th February.

● The following day, Buller managed to cross the Tugela River and relieved the siege at Ladysmith. Bloemfontein, the capital of the Orange Free State, also fell to the British.

- Mafeking was relieved on 17th May, and was held up as an example of British courage and resolve. The British commander there, Colonel Robert Baden-Powell, had withstood the siege with only a small force for 217 days.

- Lord Roberts marched into Pretoria, the capital of the Transvaal, on 5th June, and President Kruger fled.

Guerrilla war and stalemate

- The British may have taken important strongholds but there were still 25,000 armed Boers hiding in the veld grasslands. These men led raids on British convoys, and blew up railway lines to stop supplies and troops from getting through.

- Lord Roberts was replaced by Lord Kitchener in December 1900. Kitchener was more ruthless than his predecessor, and sanctioned the burning of Boer farms and villages.

- Concentration camps were set up to house Boer women and children whose husbands and fathers were still fighting.

- Word spread of the appalling conditions in the camps. An anti-war campaigner named Emily Hobhouse saw them and wrote a damning account, which whipped up public opinion and forced the government to improve conditions. In all, around 28,000 Boers, mostly children, died in the camps, and it is possible that a further 20,000 black Africans died, too.

- Slowly the Boer commandos in the field began to run out of supplies. The British showed no signs of giving up and eventually even the Boer generals were calling for peace.

- In May 1902, the remaining Boer fighters agreed to surrender.

Consequences of the Boer War

- The British had lost close to 100,000 men during the Boer campaign. The Boers lost around 7,000 soldiers and 28,000 civilians.

- The Transvaal and Orange Free State were taken and rebuilt by the British and, along with the Cape Colony, formed into the Union of South Africa in 1910.

- The British had found that their army was not as effective fighting a large campaign, having grown used to small colonial conflicts in the past. Lessons were learned and reforms made to make the military more efficient.

- Britain had also relied heavily on its Empire to fight the war, as no help was forthcoming from other strong powers, such as Russia or France. This encouraged Britain to create alliances with these countries to make its military position stronger for the future.

⟨✓⟩ You will need to recall the timelines of the Indian Mutiny and the Anglo-Boer War. Draw each one as a flowchart in chronological order and include what sparked the conflict (new cartridges for the sepoys in India), the crucial battles fought and their outcomes (e.g. Magersfontein and Spion Kop), and the consequences of British victory.

Summary

You should now know the following:

1.   The background to British rule in India.

2.   The key causes, events and consequences of the Indian Mutiny of 1857.

3.   The background to British rule in South Africa.

4.   The key causes, events and consequences of the Anglo-Boer War of 1899–1902.

Test yourself

Before moving on to the next chapter, make sure you can answer the following questions. The answers are at the back of the book.

1.   Which British military leader won the Battle of Plassey in 1757?

2.   Who was the Mughal Emperor at the time of the Indian Mutiny?

3.   By what term did the Boers refer to outsiders living in the Transvaal?

4.   At which siege did General Cronje surrender his Boer soldiers in 1900?

Sample question answers

These suggested answers to the sample essay questions are intended to provide pointers to the way you structure your answers in the exam. Check your answers against these points. You will be expected to write your answers in **full prose** and marks may be awarded for the quality of your writing.

Chapter 1

(a)   Describe the main events of the year 1066.   (20)

- Edward the Confessor died on 5th January. Harold Godwinson was chosen as King by the Witan and crowned the following day.

- Harold knew that Duke William of Normandy would attempt an invasion of England and spent the year preparing for it.

- Harold placed his troops along the south coast of England and left Earls Edwin and Morcar to guard the north.

- Meanwhile, in Normandy, William convinced his nobles to support an invasion of England and gained the support of Pope Alexander II.

- William gathered an army and ordered a fleet of ships to be built. He then had to wait until late September for the right wind to allow them to sail across the Channel.

- An army from Norway, led by Harald Hardrada, arrived in the north of England and defeated Edwin and Morcar at the Battle of Fulford on 20th September.

- Harold marched his army north and defeated Hardrada at the Battle of Stamford Bridge on 25th September.

- William landed in the south on 28th September, forcing Harold to march his exhausted army back down south.

- Harold and William met on Senlac Hill outside Hastings on 14th October. There, after a battle lasting all day, Harold was killed and the English were defeated.

- William then marched to London, gained the support of the nobility and was crowned King on 25th December.

(b)   Explain the reasons why Harold lost the Battle of Hastings.   (10)

- Harold lost the Battle of Hastings due to bad luck, poor discipline in his fyrd and the superiority of the Norman cavalry.

- Harold was unlucky in that the Normans landed on an undefended coast while his army were in the north. After fighting a battle, Harold's army then had to march quickly down to Hastings and fight another straight away.

- The English fyrd were ill-disciplined in that they allowed the shieldwall to break up. When the Bretons on the left flank of William's army retreated, the English broke rank and ran after them. If the shieldwall had held, the English might not have suffered so many casualties.

- With the shieldwall weakened, it collapsed under the Norman onslaught and Harold was killed in the fighting.

Chapter 2

(a)   Describe the threats to his rule that William I faced.   (20)

- The English earls Edwin and Morcar rebelled against William in 1069.

- They were aided in their rebellion by some Vikings and Scots.

- The Norman soldiers stationed at York were killed.

- In response, William ordered his soldiers to lay waste to large areas of Yorkshire. The people were killed, their homes looted and land burned.

- This has become known as the 'Harrying of the North'.

- An Englishman called Hereward the Wake led revolts in East Anglia.

- Hereward has become a legendary folk figure.

(b)   Explain the steps that William took to gain control over the English people.   (10)

- William introduced the Feudal System to England. This was a series of agreements of loyalty, which ran from the King down to the peasants.

- The nobles under the King were obliged to provide a number of men for military service.

- The Feudal System assured William of his nobles' loyalty and guaranteed that they could gather him an army.

- The 'Harrying of the North' in 1069 was a brutal method of control – it effectively wiped out large areas of resistance.

- The Normans also introduced new castles to England. These were motte and baileys that could be built quickly and cheaply.

- Positions of authority, such as earls and bishops, were filled by Normans.

- By compiling the Domesday Book, William was able to find out exactly how many soldiers he could hope to gather for an army.

Chapter 3

(a) Describe the typical day of a monk or nun in a monastery or nunnery.   (20)

- At midnight a monk would attend the service of Matins for an hour, then go back to bed until 6 am for the service of Prime.

- After Prime there was breakfast, then work or study, followed by Chapter Mass at 9 am and a session in the Chapter House for the administration of the monastery.

- At 11 am there was High Mass, then lunch at noon and a rest until 2 pm.

- Nones followed and then work, followed by Vespers at 4 pm and more work.

- Supper was eaten at 6 pm and then the service of Compline at 7 pm, followed by bed.

(b) Explain the effect that monasteries had on society and how society could affect them.   (10)

- Monasteries provided relief for the poor by giving them food, and to travellers by providing them with shelter.

- Youngsters who joined the order would receive a good education from the monastery's many books, which were copied by the monks.

- Local people could be employed as servants if the monastery was wealthy.

- The locals might also pay money to the monastery because they believed that this would help them to reach Heaven.

- However, a monastery that was too wealthy might allow the rules of St Benedict, which promoted poverty, to be forgotten.

Chapter 4

(a) Describe the events that led to Henry II's falling-out with Thomas Beckett.   (20)

- Henry II drew up the Constitutions of Clarendon in 1164, which stated that no one could be excommunicated, no churchman could leave England without his permission and that criminous clerks should be tried in royal courts, rather than Church courts.

- Becket opposed these rules and refused to accept them.

- Becket went to France for five years and Henry seized his lands. In the meantime, Henry wanted to crown his son Henry King of England and tried to use Archbishop Roger of York to carry out the ceremony.

- The Pope intervened and forced Henry to make peace with Becket, who returned to England in 1170.

- Becket then excommunicated everyone involved in the coronation.

- It was then that Henry is said to have shouted 'Will no one rid me of this turbulent priest?', which prompted four knights to travel to England and murder Becket.

(b) Which man – Henry or Thomas – do you think was more to blame for what happened? Explain your answer. (10)

- Henry II wanted the Constitutions of Clarendon passed because of his greed. He wanted criminous clerks to be tried in royal courts so that he, rather than the Church, could collect any fines that were paid. When Becket went to France, he seized all his lands and held them for himself.

- Henry had a violent temper, which is shown in his conduct towards Becket. It was his rash outburst in 1170 that led to Becket's murder.

- Becket was stubborn and unwilling to compromise. He refused to accept the Constitutions of Clarendon in 1164. On his return to England in 1170, he immediately excommunicated everyone involved in the coronation of Henry's son, despite knowing that it would anger the King.

[You could make a reasonable argument that either man was more responsible for what happened. But a balanced answer will add that neither man can be entirely free of blame.]

Chapter 8

(a) Describe the events of the Peasants' Revolt in 1381. (20)

- The Peasants' Revolt began in the south-east of England, from where the rebels marched to London in June 1381. They demanded to speak to the King.

- Richard II agreed to speak to the rebels at Mile End on 14th June. He told them that in future they would be fairly paid and that no one would be punished for the revolt.

- Despite this, some rebels kidnapped the Archbishop of Canterbury and the King's Treasurer and executed them.

- Richard met the rebels again at Smithfield the following day. A rebel leader named Wat Tyler was insulted by one of Richard's supporters and Tyler was killed in a scuffle.

- The King then urged the rebels to give up their cause and follow him, saying that his promises would be kept. However, the other rebel leaders were captured and executed.

(b) Explain the reasons why the peasants marched on London. (10)

- The government introduced a Poll Tax in 1377. This was repeated in 1379 and again in 1381.

- By 1381, the Poll Tax had been raised to one shilling, which most peasants could not hope to afford. This was especially the case with villeins, who were not paid for working on the land.

- The peasants took out their frustrations on the tax collectors. Soon the discontent spread to the counties surrounding London in the south-east and some government agents were killed.

- The rebels were encouraged to march by leaders such as Wat Tyler from Kent.

- The peasants marched on London mostly because of high tax rises. But they had been demanding to be paid for some years and were now beginning to question why people in authority had more rights than they had. Some no longer wanted to support the war in France or the authority of the Church.

Chapter 9

(a)   Describe the events of Henry V's French campaign of 1415, up to just before the Battle of Agincourt.   (20)

- Henry V landed in Normandy with his army in August 1415. They planned to use a *chevauchée* (a fast hit-and-run raid) to work their way deep into France.

- The English besieged the town of Harfleur, which had strong defences and did not fall until September.

- Meanwhile, the English army had become sick with dysentery, leading Henry to call off the planned raid into France. Instead, they marched along the coast towards Calais, intending to return home.

- The French marched north and attempted to block and destroy the English before they reached Calais.

- The English were held up trying to cross the River Somme but continued to march north. They found their path blocked by the French just outside the town of Agincourt on 24th October.

(b)   Explain why Henry V was successful at Agincourt.   (10)

- The battlefield at Agincourt worked in Henry's favour. It was narrow, with woods on either side, which did not allow the vast French ranks to spread out evenly.

- The field was also muddy, which hampered the advancing French army, while the English had only to hold firm in their position.

- The French soldiers wore heavy plate armour which made it difficult to get up once they had fallen down. As a result, many were trampled or drowned in the mud, forming piles of bodies, which further slowed the French advance.

- Despite being hugely outnumbered, the English soldiers were well trained. The skilful archers could also fight hand to hand, which was effective once the French had reached the English line.

Chapter 10

(a)   Describe the events that led to Edward IV gaining the throne in 1461.   (20)

- Edward IV was the son of Richard, Duke of York, who was appointed Protector in 1453, but declared a traitor in 1459.

- In response, Richard sent Yorkist forces to England and captured Henry VI.

- Henry and Richard agreed to the Act of Accord in October 1460, which declared that Richard would become King after Henry's death.

- Queen Margaret opposed this, and the Lancastrians defeated and killed Richard at the Battle of Wakefield in December 1460. Henry VI was freed after a similar defeat at St Albans in February 1461.

- Edward marched towards London with another force of Yorkists from the West Country. They were able to enter the city, which the Lancastrians had been unable to do.

- Edward then marched after the Lancastrians and met them in battle at Towton in March 1461.

- The Lancastrians were crushed at Towton and Edward was crowned King Edward IV.

(b)   Explain why Henry VI was able to regain the throne in 1470.   (10)

- Henry VI was able to reclaim the English throne largely because previous important supporters of Edward IV deserted him.

- Richard Neville, the Earl of Warwick, was Edward's cousin and fought for the Yorkists. However, he fell out with the King when Edward married into the Woodville family, who were rivals to the Neville family. Warwick felt that he was losing influence at court.

- Edward's brother, George, Duke of Clarence, also turned against him. Clarence plotted with Warwick to remove Edward from the throne. Although their attempt was unsuccessful, when the pair fled to France they were able to offer their support to Henry VI.

- When the combined Lancastrian forces of Henry VI, Queen Margaret, Warwick and Clarence invaded England in 1470, Edward judged that the threat to him was too severe. He fled England and Henry VI was allowed to re-take the throne.

Chapter 11

(a)   Describe the ways in which Henry VII controlled his nobility.   (20)

- Henry VII replaced Yorkist nobles with those who had supported him. Lancastrian nobles who had had their lands taken by Edward IV now had them restored.

- The Court of Star Chamber was set up to deal with any rebellion provoked by the nobility. The court could confiscate land and issue fines.

- Justices of the Peace were appointed all over the country to keep order and promote the courts outside of London.

- The Law of Livery restricted nobles from retaining a large private army. They also had to sign a recognisance by which they agreed to give up a sum of money if they were disloyal.

- The influence of the nobility was removed from the government as Henry appointed lesser members of the gentry to his Council and to run the court system.

- The Council of Wales and Council of the North were formed to take care of areas where the nobles were not as supportive of Henry.

(b) Explain how these actions helped Henry hold on to the throne. (10)

- Henry needed to control his nobles because he recognised that a strong nobility would pose more of a threat if it turned against him.

- Loyal nobles were encouraged to stay loyal by the threat of severe punishment if they rebelled. The most loyal were rewarded with gifts of land that had been taken from Yorkists.

- The removal of nobles from Henry's Council meant that he could now rely on the advice of educated men in dealing with threats to his rule.

- The courts' use of fines raised a lot of money for the royal treasury – sufficient for the King to raise a strong army if he needed to.

- The Council of Wales and Council of the North, as well as the appointment of Justices of the Peace, meant that the King had some sort of royal presence everywhere in the country.

Chapter 12

(a) Describe the events of the Pilgrimage of Grace. (20)

- At Lincoln in 1536, 10,000 men attacked the commissioners looking to dissolve the monasteries and occupied the cathedral.

- In Yorkshire, Robert Aske and Lord Darcy gathered together a force of 30,000 men.

- In December, Aske drew up a petition calling for an end to heresy. Aske also declared Princess Mary to be legitimate.

- The men marched south towards London. They claimed that they did not mean to attack the King, but rather free him from the influence of heretical advisors. For this reason, they argued, their movement should be seen as a pilgrimage rather than a rebellion.

- They were met at Doncaster by the Duke of Norfolk, who promised that their complaints would be heard in Parliament.

- However, these promises were not kept, and the leaders of the pilgrimage were captured and executed.

(b) Explain why the rebels were not able to succeed. (10)

- The Pilgrimage of Grace did not succeed because the rebels underestimated the ruthlessness of Henry VIII and Cromwell, and their unwillingness to negotiate about religious matters.

- The Dissolution of the Monasteries was necessary both to raise money for the royal treasury and to continue the process of removing Catholic practices from England. Henry and Cromwell were therefore unlikely to abandon it.

- Princess Mary was declared illegitimate because Henry wanted his marriage to Catherine of Aragon to be annulled. This was done in the hope that he could marry again and produce a son. To reverse the decision without a male heir, would have undone all of his efforts to secure the succession.

- The rebels believed Norfolk's promises that their cause would be debated in Parliament. They underestimated Henry's brutality and believed that they would escape punishment by claiming to be on a pilgrimage rather than part of a rebellion.

Chapter 14

(a) Describe the main events of the Elizabethan Settlement. (20)

- The key points of the Elizabethan Settlement were set out in two Acts of Parliament in 1559: the Act of Supremacy and the Act of Uniformity; and then by the Thirty-Nine Articles, passed in 1571.

- The Act of Supremacy established Elizabeth as the Supreme Governor of the Church of England.

- The Act of Uniformity introduced a new version of the *Book of Common Prayer*, based on the 1552 version by Thomas Cranmer.

- Priests now had to wear vestments and people were compelled to attend church on Sundays or risk being fined.

- The Thirty-Nine Articles got rid of certain key Catholic beliefs such as transubstantiation and allowed priests to marry.

(b) Explain how Elizabeth hoped to appeal to both moderate Catholics and Protestants. (10)

- In 1559, the Elizabethan Settlement took a central line that Elizabeth hoped would appeal to both moderate Protestants and moderate Catholics.

- The Act of Supremacy stated that Elizabeth was Supreme Governor of the Church, but stopped short of naming her as head of the Church. This allowed Catholics to believe that this position was still held by the Pope.

- The Act of Uniformity introduced a Prayer Book based on Cranmer's Protestant 1552 version. But it made priests wear vestments to appeal to the Catholic view – although these were slightly toned down.

- In dealing with transubstantiation, the new Prayer Book used wording vague enough to allow the people to view it in accordance with their own beliefs.

Chapter 15

(a)   Describe the process of enclosure.   (20)

- Enclosure was a process that allowed a change in land use from arable farming to pastoral farming.

- First, the open fields were divided into separate areas. Second, the common land of each manor was fenced off.

- In medieval times each manor had open fields, upon which the peasants each farmed a strip. Enclosure meant that the lords divided the whole field into smaller fields for grazing animals.

- The area of common land in each manor used to be available for all the people to graze whatever animals they had. Enclosure meant that the lords took these for themselves and used them to graze their own livestock.

- The process of enclosure was characterised by the erection of permanent fences and walls, either to divide up the large open fields or to fence off the old common land from the people.

(b)   Explain why this process led to unrest in the countryside.   (10)

- The enclosure movement led to unrest in the countryside because the peasants found themselves either without jobs or without land to farm themselves.

- Some peasants relied on renting land from their lords, to produce their own crops to eat, sell or feed to their animals. This land was taken away and the peasants were left without access to food.

- Pastoral farming was not as labour intensive, meaning that fewer men were needed to do the work. The peasants who worked their lords' land for pay, found themselves without a source of income.

- The loss of the common land meant that any peasants who owned animals no longer had any land on which to graze them. The animals could not exercise or grow effectively, and another source of food and income was lost.

- The discontent over enclosure led to uprisings such as Kett's Rebellion in 1549.

Chapter 17

(a) Describe the main events of Oliver Cromwell's rule as Lord Protector. (20)

- When Oliver Cromwell was appointed Lord Protector he intended to rule closely with Parliament. However, he decided to call in the army instead when certain MPs threatened to support the restoration of the monarchy.

- In 1655, Cromwell divided England into 11 districts and appointed a Major-General to each one. The Major-Generals were responsible for keeping law and order in their districts.

- Cromwell raised a ten per cent tax called the decimation tax to help finance the local armies in each district.

- Cromwell banned unlawful assemblies and the owning of weapons by known Royalists, and called for robbers and vagrants to be severely punished.

- Cromwell also continued to introduce laws that made people's way of life as Puritan as possible. Entertainment and alcohol were banned, as was the celebration of 'Catholic' festivals such as Christmas.

- In 1657, Cromwell met with the army to draw up a new constitution for England. Later that year he was formally sworn in as Lord Protector, in a magnificent ceremony.

(b) Explain why there might have been opposition to the ceremony appointing Cromwell as Lord Protector in 1657. (10)

- Cromwell's appointment as Lord Protector was not formalised until 1657, after he discussed a new English constitution with his army leaders.

- The army leaders did not want Cromwell to be sworn in to his position in the same manner as a king.

- There was a strong opinion that Cromwell should not be seen as a replacement for Charles I, whom they had fought so hard to get rid of. The army believed that, once Cromwell was dead, this might encourage Charles's son to continue his efforts to reclaim the throne.

- Any opposition to the ceremony in 1657 would have been because it was very similar to a king's coronation. It was a magnificent occasion with much wealth on display, which many would have believed to have gone against Cromwell's Puritan principles.

Chapter 19

(a) Describe the events leading to the Act of Union in 1707. (20)

- In the years leading up to 1707, Scotland felt that it was being marginalised by England. The Scots were not seeing a share of the wealth that Britain was gaining through overseas trade.

- Scottish merchants were banned from trading in places where English companies had a monopoly.

- Anne was worried that the Scots, who had not supported England in the recent war, would form an alliance with France.

- The Scots did not agree with the Hanoverian succession and wanted to debate their right to choose their own monarch.

- It was therefore agreed that the English and Scottish Parliaments should merge to debate these important issues. This happened with the passing of the Act of Union in May 1707.

(b) Explain why there was both opposition and support for this Act in Scotland. (10)

- The Scots supported the Act of Union because it gave them an equal share in the wealth obtained through Britain's trade.

- Scotland was also allowed to keep its own Presbyterian church, which did not have bishops and was entirely separate from the Church of England.

- However, the Scots who opposed the Hanoverian succession and only wanted to debate it with the English Parliament found that they had to accept it as they were 'tied' to England.

- Any hope of an alliance with France, which was traditionally a strong ally of Scotland, was lost.

Chapter 20

(a) Describe the main events of the 1745 Jacobite Rebellion. (20)

- Charles Edward Stuart, in exile in France, sailed to Scotland and landed on the island of Eriksay in July 1745. He marched across the Highlands, gathering support as he went.

- Charles's army defeated a government army at the Battle of Prestonpans in September 1745. They then marched south, across the border and into England.

- The Jacobites reached Derby, but were persuaded to turn back due to lack of support. They received reinforcements in Scotland and won another battle against a government army at Falkirk in January 1746.

- A new government army, led by William, Duke of Cumberland, marched north and met the Jacobites on Culloden Moor on 16th April 1746.

- During the battle that followed, the well-trained government soldiers were able to defeat the undisciplined Highlanders. The Jacobites scattered all over Scotland and Charles fled back to France.

- Over the next few months, the government soldiers rampaged through the Highlands, putting down any sign of resistance and rounding up any known Jacobites.

(b)   Explain why the rebellion was not successful.   (10)

- The 1745 Jacobite Rebellion was not successful because of the inability of the Jacobites to gain widespread support, Charles Edward Stuart's inexperience in battle and the superiority of the government army under the Duke of Cumberland.

- When Charles first marched through Scotland he was able to gain the support of several Scottish clans. But many others remained loyal and some even fought on the government side at Culloden.

- The Jacobites were unable to gain further support during the march south through England. There may have been sympathetic English Catholics who were simply unwilling to accept him as King.

- Charles was inexperienced but stubborn. He refused to listen to his generals at Culloden, who advised him to avoid battle until they found a location more suited to them. His successes at Prestonpans and Falkirk had made him over-confident.

- The government army at Culloden was far superior in its tactics, discipline and fighting skills. While the Highlanders charged in a disorganised manner, the government soldiers were well trained and held their positions.

Chapter 21

(a)   Describe the events in America between 1750 and 1755.   (20)

- The British had established several communities of settlers along the eastern coast of America.

- The French also had settlers in Canada.

- In the early 1750s the French settlers tried to move southwards into the British colonies.

- They aimed for Virginia, New York and Georgia, and built forts along the Appalachian Mountains.

- War broke out between Britain and France when the Virginia militia, led by George Washington, attempted to capture the French Fort Duquesne in 1754.

- General Braddock led another attempt to take Fort Duquesne in 1755.

- The British were defeated by the French and a tribe of Native Americans at the Battle of Monongahela River.

(b)   Explain the reasons why these events led to the outbreak of war.   (10)

- The British claimed that the French had invaded their American colonies when French settlers moved there and built forts.

- Nonetheless, the conflict remained in America for the moment, handled by the colonial militias.

- When the attempt was made to capture Fort Duquesne in 1754 the French regarded it as an act of war.

- Both sides sent troops from home to reinforce the militias in their colonies.

Chapter 22

(a) Describe the events of the later American War of Independence between 1778 and 1883. (20)

- General Lord Cornwallis was able to regain British control over Georgia, South Carolina and North Carolina.

- The British won the Battle of Guilford Courthouse in 1781.

- Cornwallis met up with Benedict Arnold, an ex-Patriot who switched sides, and they settled their troops in Yorktown.

- George Washington marched into Virginia and trapped the British on Yorktown's peninsula.

- Meanwhile, a French fleet drove the British ships away from Chesapeake Bay.

- The British surrendered on 19th October 1781 and began to bring their troops home.

- The Peace of Paris was signed in 1783 and ended the fighting in America.

(b) Explain why these events led to a British defeat. (10)

- The British believed that Loyalists in the southern colonies would support them against the Patriots.

- However, there were not as many Loyalists willing to do this as the British hoped.

- Once the British defeated an army and moved away, they were unable to maintain British rule there.

- George Washington was able to sneak up on Cornwallis and Arnold at Yorktown.

- He fooled General Clinton into believing that he was going to attack New York, rather than march south into Virginia.

- Washington was also able to make his march coincide with French naval activities in Chesapeake Bay.

Chapter 26

(a) Describe the key developments in the coming of the railways. (20)

- The development of the railways came because of developments in the manufacture of iron and the use of steam power.

- Richard Trevithick made a locomotive that pulled wagons between Merthyr Tydfil and the Glamorganshire Canal in 1804.

- Trevithick also built the *Catch-Me-Who-Can* in 1808, which gave rides to passengers on a circular track.

- George Stephenson built both the Stockton and Darlington, and Liverpool and Manchester railways.

- Stephenson's *Rocket* won the Rainhill Trials, held to determine whether steam was best to power the locomotives, in October 1829.

(b) Explain why the railways were so important to the country as a whole. (10)

- In the 20 years after the opening of the Liverpool and Manchester railway in 1830, over 6,000 miles of railway line were laid in Britain.

- Railways began to replace road and canal transportation for goods. They were faster, more efficient and, as the rail network grew, trains could go further afield.

- People also began to travel more by train and journey times to destinations were greatly reduced.

- Railways allowed people to commute to work and to take holidays.

Chapter 28

(a) Describe the purpose and approach of the Great Exhibition. (20)

- The idea behind the Great Exhibiton was to show the successes of Britain and its Empire, both to the British people and to the whole world.

- It was housed in an iconic building, designed by the architect Joseph Paxton, that became known as the Crystal Palace.

- The Crystal Palace in Hyde Park was 563m long and 139m wide, and enclosed a whole row of elm trees.

- The exhibition was divided between exhibits on Britain and the Empire, and the rest of the world.

- The admittance charge was £3, but on certain days admittance could be gained for one shilling.

- The Great Exhibition admitted 500,000 people on its opening day, 1st May 1851, when it was attended by Queen Victoria and Prince Albert.

(b) Explain its importance and success to the country as a whole. (10)

- Between May and October 1851, four million people attended the Great Exhibition.

- The 'shilling days' allowed the lower classes to attend and communities organised trips to London to visit as a group.

- The classes were able to mix as they had not done before, and Queen Victoria was known to sometimes attend to see all classes of British people.

- On the initiative of Prince Albert, the profits made by the Great Exhibition were invested into cultural foundations in London.

- The Royal Albert Hall, and the Victoria and Albert, Natural History and Science Museums, were all formed using this money.

Chapter 29

(a) Describe the life and achievements of William Gladstone.   (20)

- William Gladstone supported Robert Peel on the repeal of the Corn Laws.

- Nonetheless, he later joined the Whigs in 1859 and formed the Liberal party. He led them to government in 1868.

- The Liberals passed a number of social reform acts, including the Elementary Education Act 1870, which made it compulsory for children to attend school until the age of 11.

- In 1886, Gladstone granted Home Rule, a limited amount of independence, to Ireland.

- Home Rule was opposed by the Conservatives and much of the Liberal Party, who split away from Gladstone.

(b) Explain why his career might be regarded as a failure by some.   (10)

- William Gladstone was a Tory and supported Robert Peel, but when he formed the Liberal Party he gave the impression that he was not fully committed to his causes.

- He did not regard social reform as very important and believed that the poor should help themselves.

- He was stubborn on the Home Rule issue, which split his party and caused power to go to the Conservatives. The Liberal Party was unelectable for many years.

- However, Gladstone did achieve several terms as Prime Minister and passed several important social reform acts, despite his personal opinion of them.

Test yourself answers

Chapter 1

1. William claimed Harold swore an oath that he would support William's claim to the English throne.

2. Tostig Godwinson supported Harald Hardrada.

3. The Witan was a council that included the most important nobles and churchmen in England.

4. The Normans landed at Pevensey on 28th September 1066.

5. The battle between Harold and William was fought at Senlac Hill, near Hastings, on 14th October 1066.

Chapter 2

1. A landholder who swore fealty became a vassal to his lord.

2. Edwin and Morcar reclaimed York from the Normans in 1069.

3. The typical features of Norman churches were thick stone walls, and rounded arches over the doors and windows.

4. The Domesday Book refers to the time in the reign of King Edward, when the land was granted by William, and at the time of the survey.

5. Cottars were paid wages to work.

6. The land belonging to the lord of the manor was known as his demesne.

Chapter 3

1. Archbishop Anselm of Canterbury quarrelled with William II.

2. Henry I had one surviving legitimate child, a daughter. He wanted her to take over the throne after him, but many nobles did not like the idea of a woman leading the country.

3. Murals were painted on church walls to give a religious message to those who could not read. The murals often depicted Hell, as a reminder of what awaited them if they sinned.

4. If a monastery became wealthy, the monks might allow themselves more luxuries. Therefore the rules of St Benedict – which urged a simple life with no possessions – would not be followed.

Chapter 4

1. The three points of the Constitutions of Clarendon that Thomas Becket refused to accept were those that stated no one could be excommunicated without the King's permission; no churchman could leave England without the King's permission; and criminous clerks would be sentenced by the royal courts.

2. The Pope objected when Henry II tried to use Archbishop Roger of York for the coronation of his son.

3. Henry II's sons Henry, Richard and Geoffrey, and their mother Eleanor of Aquitaine, were all involved in the 1173 revolt against the King.

Chapter 5

1. The crusaders captured Antioch in 1098.

2. The terms of the 1192 truce stated that Richard could keep all the land he had conquered down to Jaffa, but everything south of the city, including Jerusalem, had to be left for Saladin.

3. Pope Innocent III placed England under an interdict in 1208.

4. The Magna Carta was presented to John at Runnymede, near Windsor, in 1215.

Chapter 6

1. Simon de Montfort was killed at the Battle of Evesham in 1265.

2. Edward I twice defeated Llewelyn of Wales by cutting off the Welsh supply line from Anglesey.

3. A Scottish rebel army led by William Wallace won the Battle of Stirling Bridge in 1297.

4. The English retreated quickly from the battlefield at Bannockburn because they thought that the Scots were receiving reinforcements. In fact, these were just ordinary people and not soldiers.

5. Roger Mortimer plotted with Isabella of France to overthrow Edward II.

Chapter 7

1. Edward I's castles in Wales were made up of concentric rings.

2. An anti-Jewish attack is called a pogrom.

3. Margaret Paston handled her husband's business during his absence.

4. *Yersinia pestis* is the bacteria that causes bubonic plague.

5. Flagellants were people who believed that by whipping themselves they would pay penance for other people's sins and therefore stop the Plague, which they saw as a punishment from God.

Chapter 8

1. The Poll Tax was raised in 1377, 1379 and 1381.

2. In 1397, Richard II dealt with the Lords Appellant by having one executed, another murdered and the other three sent into exile.

3. An apprentice was held in the service of a master craftsman by an agreement called an indenture.

4. A charter was needed for a town to appoint its own government.

Chapter 9

1. Owain Glyndwr fought at the Battle of Shrewsbury in 1403.

2. A swift attack with horses for pillage was called a *chevauchée*.

3. Joan of Arc was convicted of being a witch, allowing the English to execute her.

4. Jack Cade led the Kentish rebellion of 1450.

Chapter 10

1. The symbols of the Yorkists and the Lancastrians were the white rose and the red rose, respectively.

2. Richard Neville, Earl of Warwick, is often known as the 'Kingmaker'.

3. Prince Edward was killed at the Battle of Tewkesbury in 1471.

4. Richard III claimed that the marriage between Edward IV and Elizabeth Woodville had been invalid. Therefore any children they had would have been illegitimate and, thus, Edward V would have been barred from the throne.

5. The Earl of Northumberland failed to come to the aid of Richard III at the Battle of Bosworth.

Chapter 11

1. Holding a personal army was called retaining.

2. Perkin Warbeck claimed to be Richard of York, the younger of the 'Princes in the Tower'.

3. Lord Audley joined the Cornish tax rebels in 1497.

4. The marriage of Arthur and Catherine of Aragon was arranged by the Treaty of Medina del Campo.

Chapter 12

1.   Benevolences were gifts of money made by the nobles to the King in order to secure their estates and positions.

2.   The meeting between Henry VIII and Francis I in June 1520 was called the 'Field of the Cloth of Gold'.

3.   Henry VIII was awarded the title *Fidei Defensor* for writing a book arguing against Martin Luther's teachings.

4.   Henry VIII wanted his marriage to Catherine of Aragon to be annulled because he wanted a male heir, which Catherine seemed unable to provide.

5.   The First Fruits and Tenths Act allowed Henry VIII to take a portion of the earnings of church offices.

6.   The Act of Ten Articles allowed the three sacraments of baptism, penance and the eucharist to be recognised.

Chapter 13

1.   John Calvin argued for a more radical form of Protestantism than Martin Luther.

2.   Lady Jane Grey unofficially reigned as Queen for nine days.

3.   Wyatt's Rebellion failed mostly because Mary was able to persuade the Londoners to remain loyal to her.

4.   John Foxe's *Acts and Monuments* (also known as the *Book of Martyrs*) recorded the execution of Protestants under Mary I.

Chapter 14

1.   The Act of Supremacy (1559) made a small concession to Catholics by referring to Elizabeth I as the Supreme Governor of the English Church, implying that the Pope still held some authority as head of the Church.

2.   Sir Francis Walsingham was the head of Elizabeth I's secret service.

3.   The Battle of Gravelines was the bloodiest of the Spanish Armada campaign in 1588.

4.   Hugh O'Neill led the Irish uprising against Elizabeth I between 1598 and 1602.

Chapter 15

1. Companies could obtain a monopoly by opening up new trade routes.

2. The deserving poor were those unable to work. The idle poor were those who did not work through laziness.

3. Enclosure encouraged the growth of the wool trade. Merchants then exported the wool to foreign countries, allowing the government to raise money through an export tax.

4. The wives of rich husbands had to supervise their servants and make sure that the household was being run properly.

Chapter 16

1. James I refused to dismiss the English bishops at the Hampton Court Palace conference in 1604.

2. The Addled Parliament of 1614 was dissolved because it would not agree to James I's request to raise taxes.

3. The ship money tax led to the trial of John Hampden.

4. Charles I attempted to arrest John Pym, John Hampden, Arthur Haselrig, Denzil Holles and William Strode.

Chapter 17

1. The Battle of Edgehill was fought on 23rd October 1642.

2. The Marquess of Newcastle commanded the 'Whitecoats' at the Battle of Marston Moor.

3. Charles I made secret negotiations with the Scots while imprisoned in Carisbrooke Castle.

4. The decimation tax financed the local armies of the Major-Generals.

5. Charles II is supposed to have hidden in an oak tree after the Battle of Worcester in 1651.

6. The Declaration of Breda set out the terms of Charles II's restoration to the throne.

Chapter 18

1. The Convention Parliament overturned all the laws of the *Interregnum*.

2. The Great Fire of London started in the bakery of Thomas Farynor on Pudding Lane.

3. Charles II converted to Catholicism on his deathbed.

4. The Monmouth Rebellion was put down at the Battle of Sedgemoor in 1685.

5. William of Orange landed at Brixham, Devon, in November 1688.

Chapter 19

1. The Toleration Act (1689) allowed people to worship in private as they wished.

2. The Battle of the Boyne was fought on 12th July 1690.

3. The German allies at the Battle of Blenheim were led by Prince Eugene of Savoy.

4. The Peace of Utrecht ended the fighting between Britain and France in 1713.

5. The Act of Union came into effect in May 1707.

Chapter 20

1. Fort William, Fort Augustus and Fort George were built after the 1715 Jacobite Rebellion.

2. Sales of shares in the South Sea Company caused a stock market crash in 1720.

3. The Treaty of Seville allowed Spanish sailors to board British vessels in Spanish waters.

4. George II led the English and Hanoverian army at the Battle of Dettingen.

5. Lord George Murray advised Bonnie Prince Charlie not to fight at Culloden.

Chapter 21

1. The British made two attempts to capture Fort Duquesne in 1754 and 1755.

2. Pitt the Elder encouraged King Frederick the Great of Prussia to fight the French in Europe.

3. General Montcalm was the French commander during the Battle of the Plains of Abraham.

4. The Peace of Paris ended the Seven Years' War in 1763.

Chapter 22

1. The British government passed the Coercive Acts in response to the Boston Tea Party.

2. Major Pitcairn commanded the British during the battles of Lexington and Concord.

3. Daniel Morgan and Benedict Arnold assisted General Gates at Bemis Heights.

4. General Cornwallis defeated General Greene at the Battle of Guilford Courthouse in 1781.

Chapter 23

1. The French Parliament called itself the National Assembly after 1789.

2. *Habeas corpus* is the rule of law which holds that people cannot be arrested and held indefinitely without a trial.

3. Napoleon destroyed most of the French ships at Aboukir Bay in 1798.

4. Nelson was hit and killed by a musket ball fired from the *Redoutable*.

5. Arthur Wellesley forced the French out of Spain at the Battle of Vitoria in 1812.

6. Napoleon Bonaparte was exiled to the island of Elba in 1812.

Chapter 24

1. The 1820 conspiracy against the British government was discovered in Cato Street, London.

2. Constituencies with a very small number of voters were called 'rotten boroughs'.

3. The Duke of Wellington attempted to form a government on the resignation of Earl Grey in 1832.

4. William Lovett published the Six Points and supported the moral force.

Chapter 25

1. Robert Bakewell experimented with selective breeding in the 1760s.

2. The process by which wrought iron is produced from pig iron is called 'puddling'.

3. John Kay invented the 'flying shuttle' in 1733.

4. Matthew Boulton went into business with the inventor James Watt.

Chapter 26

1. The 'Rebecca Riots' took place in South Wales between 1839 and 1844.

2. Canal building in Britain stopped during the late 18th century because of the war in France.

3. The Liverpool and Manchester railway opened in September 1830.

4. The Clifton Suspension Bridge in Bristol was designed by Brunel.

Chapter 27

1. Granville Sharp was instrumental in first pressing for the abolition of slavery.

2. The Dolben Act prevented too many slaves from being carried on a ship.

3. Ladies' Committees were groups founded by Elizabeth Fry that visited women's prisons.

4. The Factory Act 1850 set the daily working hours for women and children as between 6am and 6pm.

Chapter 28

1. The building housing the Great Exhibition was called the Crystal Palace.

2. The Battle of Balaklava was fought on 25th October 1854.

3. Mary Seacole set up the British Hotel near Sevastopol.

4. Florence Nightingale was given the nickname the 'Lady with the Lamp'.

Chapter 29

1. Prince Albert died in 1861.

2. The Bedchamber Crisis was caused by Victoria's refusal to change her household staff.

3. The Elementary Education Act 1870 established free schooling for children.

4. Britain gained Cyprus from Turkey in 1878.

Chapter 30

1. Robert Clive won the Battle of Plassey in 1757.

2. Bahadur Shah II was the Mughal Emperor at the time of the Indian Mutiny.

3. The Boers referred to outsiders living in the Transvaal as 'Uitlanders'.

4. General Cronje surrendered his Boer soldiers at the siege of Paardeberg in 1900.

Appendix 1 – Timelines

The monarchs of England, 1066–1485

Year	Monarch
1066	Harold II (Godwinson), Jan–Oct 1066
	William I 'The Conqueror', 1066–1087
	William II 'Rufus', 1087–1100
1100	
	Henry I 'Beauclerc', 1100–1135
	Stephen, 1135–1154
1150	
	Henry II, 1154–1189
1200	Richard I 'The Lionheart', 1189–1199
	John 'Lackland', 1199–1216
	Henry III, 1216–1272
1250	
	Edward I 'Longshanks', 1272–1307
1300	
	Edward II, 1307–1327
	Edward III, 1327–1377
1350	
	Richard II, 1377–1399
1400	Henry IV (Bolingbroke), 1399–1413
	Henry V, 1413–1422
	Henry VI, 1422–1461
1450	
	Edward IV, 1461–1470
	Henry VI, 1470–1471
	Edward IV, 1471–1483
	Edward V, April–June 1483 (not crowned)
	Richard III, 1483–1485
1500	Henry VII (Tudor), 1485–1509

The monarchs of England, 1485–1750

1485

1500   Henry VII (Tudor), 1485–1509

1550   Henry VIII, 1509–1547

              Edward VI, 1547–1553
              Mary I, 1553–1558

              Elizabeth I, 1558–1603

1600

              James I, 1603–1625

              Charles I, 1625–1649

1650   *Interregnum.* Lords Protector: Oliver Cromwell, 1653–1658
                                                   Richard Cromwell, 1658–1659

              Charles II, 1660–1685

              James II, 1685–1688
              William III, 1689–1702
              and Mary II, 1689–1694

1700   Anne, 1702–1714

              George I, 1714–1727

              George II, 1727–1760

1750

The monarchs of Great Britain and the United Kingdom, 1750–1900

George II, 1727–1760

George III, 1760–1820

George IV, 1820–1830

William IV, 1830–1837

Victoria, 1837–1901

✓ To help you remember the kings and queens of England, there is an old childhood rhyme:

Willie, Willie, Harry, Ste,
Harry, Dick, John, Harry three;
One, two, three Neds, Richard two,
Harrys four, five, six ... then who?
Edwards four, five, Dick the bad,
Harrys (twain*), then Ned (the lad);
Mary, Bessie, James the vain,
Charlie, Charlie, James again.
Will and Mary, Anna Gloria,
Georges four, then Will, Victoria;
Edward seven, George and Ted,
George the sixth, now Liz instead.

* Note that twain means two.

Learn this by heart and you will never forget who ruled when ever again.

Appendix 2 – Family trees

Dates of reigns are given in bold

For Chapters 1–2

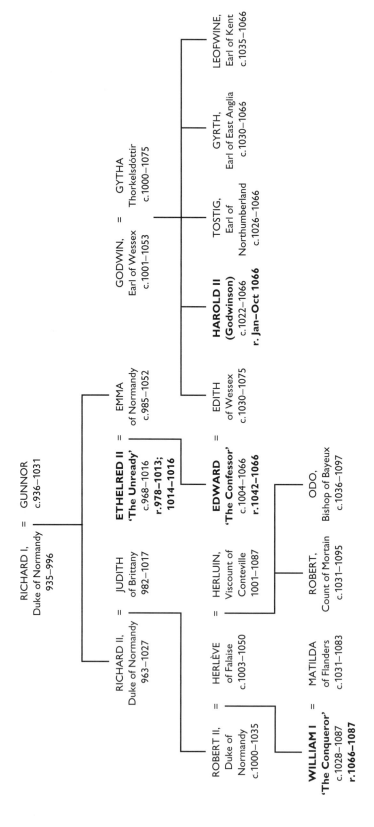

RICHARD I,
Duke of Normandy
935–996
= GUNNOR
c.936–1031

RICHARD II,
Duke of Normandy
963–1027
= JUDITH
of Brittany
982–1017

ETHELRED II
'The Unready'
c.968–1016
**r.978–1013;
1014–1016**
= EMMA
of Normandy
c.985–1052

GODWIN,
Earl of Wessex
c.1001–1053
= GYTHA
Thorkelsdóttir
c.1000–1075

ROBERT II,
Duke of
Normandy
c.1000–1035
= HERLÈVE
of Falaise
c.1003–1050

HERLUIN,
Viscount of
Conteville
1001–1087

EDWARD
'The Confessor'
c.1004–1066
r.1042–1066
= EDITH
of Wessex
c.1030–1075

HAROLD II
(Godwinson)
c.1022–1066
r. Jan–Oct 1066

TOSTIG,
Earl of
Northumberland
c.1026–1066

GYRTH,
Earl of East Anglia
c.1030–1066

LEOFWINE,
Earl of Kent
c.1035–1066

WILLIAM I
'The Conqueror'
c.1028–1087
r.1066–1087
= MATILDA
of Flanders
c.1031–1083

ROBERT,
Count of Mortain
c.1031–1095

ODO,
Bishop of Bayeux
c.1036–1097

For Chapters 3–5

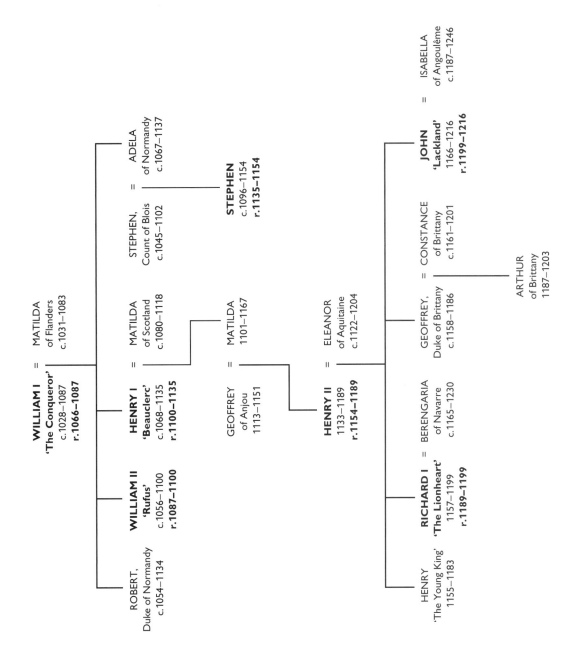

ROBERT,
Duke of Normandy
c.1054–1134

WILLIAM I
'The Conqueror'
c.1028–1087
r.1066–1087
=
MATILDA
of Flanders
c.1031–1083

WILLIAM II
'Rufus'
c.1056–1100
r.1087–1100

HENRY I
'Beauclerc'
c.1068–1135
r.1100–1135
=
MATILDA
of Scotland
c.1080–1118

ADELA
of Normandy
c.1067–1137
=
STEPHEN,
Count of Blois
c.1045–1102

STEPHEN
c.1096–1154
r.1135–1154

GEOFFREY
of Anjou
1113–1151
=
MATILDA
1101–1167

HENRY II
1133–1189
r.1154–1189
=
ELEANOR
of Aquitaine
c.1122–1204

HENRY
'The Young King'
1155–1183

RICHARD I
'The Lionheart'
1157–1199
r.1189–1199
=
BERENGARIA
of Navarre
c.1165–1230

GEOFFREY,
Duke of Brittany
c.1158–1186
=
CONSTANCE
of Brittany
c.1161–1201

JOHN
'Lackland'
1166–1216
r.1199–1216
=
ISABELLA
of Angoulême
c.1187–1246

ARTHUR
of Brittany
1187–1203

For Chapter 6

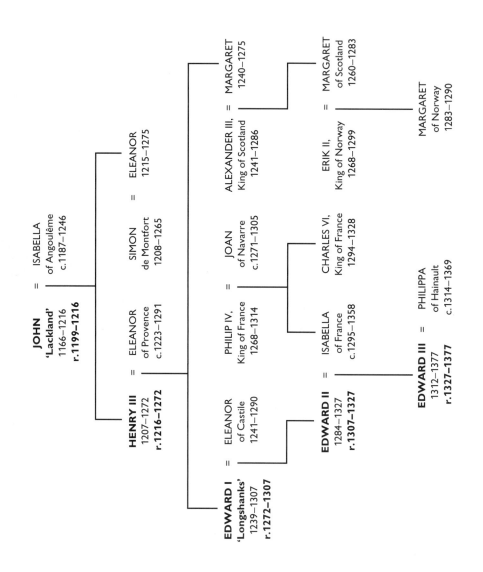

JOHN 'Lackland' 1166–1216 r.1199–1216 = ISABELLA of Angoulême c.1187–1246

HENRY III 1207–1272 r.1216–1272 = ELEANOR of Provence c.1223–1291

ELEANOR 1215–1275 = SIMON de Montfort 1208–1265

EDWARD I 'Longshanks' 1239–1307 r.1272–1307 = ELEANOR of Castile 1241–1290

EDWARD II 1284–1327 r.1307–1327 = ISABELLA of France c.1295–1358

PHILIP IV, King of France 1268–1314 = JOAN of Navarre c.1271–1305

CHARLES VI, King of France 1294–1328

ALEXANDER III, King of Scotland 1241–1286 = MARGARET 1240–1275

EDWARD III 1312–1377 r.1327–1377 = PHILIPPA of Hainault c.1314–1369

ERIK II, King of Norway 1268–1299 = MARGARET of Scotland 1260–1283

MARGARET of Norway 1283–1290

For Chapters 8–11

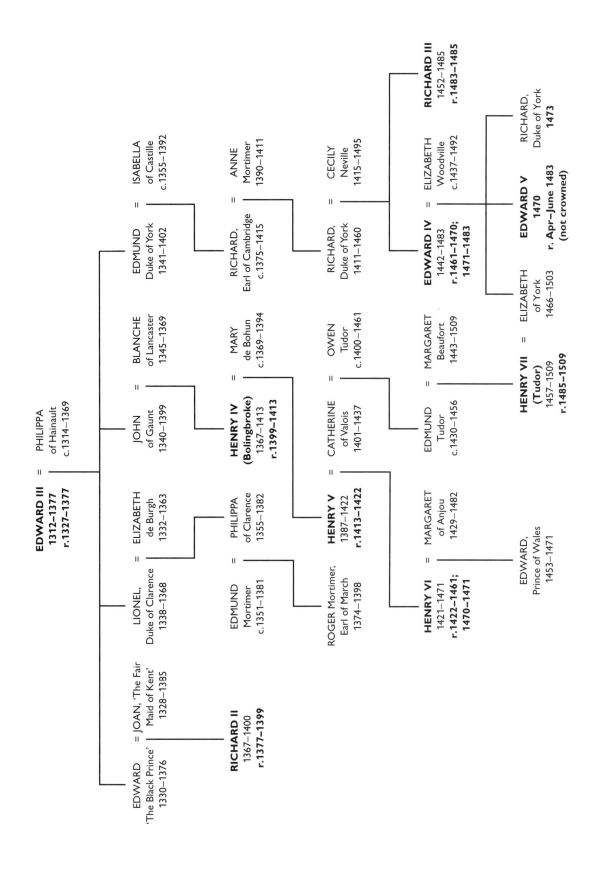

EDWARD III
1312–1377
r.1327–1377
= PHILIPPA
of Hainault
c.1314–1369

EDWARD
'The Black Prince'
1330–1376
= JOAN, 'The Fair
Maid of Kent'
1328–1385

RICHARD II
1367–1400
r.1377–1399

LIONEL,
Duke of Clarence
1338–1368
= ELIZABETH
de Burgh
1332–1363

JOHN
of Gaunt
1340–1399
= BLANCHE
of Lancaster
1345–1369

EDMUND,
Duke of York
1341–1402
= ISABELLA
of Castille
c.1355–1392

PHILIPPA
of Clarence
1355–1382
= EDMUND
Mortimer
c.1351–1381

HENRY IV
(Bolingbroke)
1367–1413
r.1399–1413
= MARY
de Bohun
c.1369–1394

RICHARD,
Earl of Cambridge
c.1375–1415
= ANNE
Mortimer
1390–1411

ROGER Mortimer,
Earl of March
1374–1398

HENRY V
1387–1422
r.1413–1422
= CATHERINE
of Valois
1401–1437
= OWEN
Tudor
c.1400–1461

RICHARD,
Duke of York
1411–1460
= CECILY
Neville
1415–1495

HENRY VI
1421–1471
r.1422–1461;
1470–1471
= MARGARET
of Anjou
1429–1482

EDMUND
Tudor
c.1430–1456
= MARGARET
Beaufort
1443–1509

EDWARD IV
1442–1483
r.1461–1470;
1471–1483
= ELIZABETH
Woodville
c.1437–1492

RICHARD III
1452–1485
r.1483–1485

EDWARD,
Prince of Wales
1453–1471

HENRY VII
(Tudor)
1457–1509
r.1485–1509
= ELIZABETH
of York
1466–1503

EDWARD V
1470
r. Apr–June 1483
(not crowned)

RICHARD,
Duke of York
1473

For Chapters 12–14

For Chapters 16–20

For Chapters 21–30

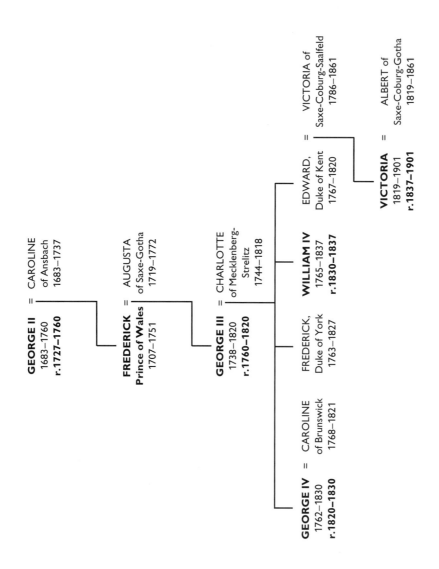

GEORGE II = CAROLINE
1683–1760   of Ansbach
r.1727–1760   1683–1737

FREDERICK = AUGUSTA
Prince of Wales   of Saxe-Gotha
1707–1751   1719–1772

GEORGE III = CHARLOTTE
1738–1820   of Mecklenberg-
r.1760–1820   Strelitz
1744–1818

GEORGE IV = CAROLINE
1762–1830   of Brunswick
r.1820–1830   1768–1821

FREDERICK,
Duke of York
1763–1827

WILLIAM IV
1765–1837
r.1830–1837

EDWARD, = VICTORIA of
Duke of Kent   Saxe-Coburg-Saalfeld
1767–1820   1786–1861

VICTORIA = ALBERT of
1819–1901   Saxe-Coburg-Gotha
r.1837–1901   1819–1861